The
Scandinavian-American
Heritage

The
Scandinavian-American
Heritage

Irene M. Franck

Part of the America's Ethnic Heritage series
General Editors: David M. Brownstone and Irene M. Franck

Facts On File Publications
New York, New York ● Oxford, England

The Scandinavian-American Heritage

Copyright © 1988 by David M. Brownstone and Irene M. Franck

Library of Congress Catalog No. 88-450-86

ISBN 0-8160-1626-7.

Series Design: Cathy Rincon

Printed in the United States of America

10 9 8 7 6 5 4 3 2 1

Contents

Preface

The Scandinavian-American Heritage is a volume in the *America's Ethnic Heritage* series, which explores the unique background of each of America's ethnic groups—their history and culture, their reasons for leaving home, their long journey to America, their waves of settlement in the new land, their often-difficult years of adjustment as they made their way into the American mainstream, and their contributions to the overall society we call "America."

We would like to thank the many people who helped us in completing this work: our expert typists, Shirley Fenn and Mary Racette; Domenico Firmani, photo researcher *par excellence*; skilled cartographer Mark Stein; James Warren, our excellent editor at Facts On File; his very able assistants, Claire Johnston and later Barbara Levine; publisher Edward Knappman, who supported the series from the start; and the many fine members of the Facts On File editorial and production staff.

Our thanks also for permission to quote two passages, on pp. x and 1, from *The People, Yes* by Carl Sandburg, copyright 1936 by Harcourt Brace Jovanovich, Inc; renewed 1964 by Carl Sandburg; reprinted by permission of the publisher.

We also express our special appreciation to the many librarians whose help has been indispensable in completing this work, especially to the incomparable staff of the Chappaqua Library—director Mark Hasskarl; the reference staff, including Mary Platt, Paula Peyraud, Terry Cullen, Martha Alcott, Carolyn Jones, and formerly Helen Barolini and Karen Baker; Jane McKean and Marcia Van Fleet and the whole circulation staff—and the many other librarians who, through the Interlibrary Loan network, have provided us with the research tools so vital to our work.

Irene M. Franck
David M. Brownstone

America's Ethnic Heritage

The United States is a great sea of peoples. All the races, nations, and beliefs of the world are met here. We live together, intermingling with each other while at the same time keeping our own separate identities. And it works. Sometimes there is pain and struggle for equality and justice, but it works—and will for as long as we all want it to.

We have brought with us to America all the ethnic heritages of the world. In that respect, there is no other place like this on Earth—no other place where all the histories of all the peoples come together. Some have therefore called the United States a great "melting pot." But that is not quite right. We do not mix and completely merge our ethnic heritages. Instead we mix them, partially merge them, and the same time keep important parts of them whole. The result is something unique called an American.

salad bowl

From six continents, seven seas, and several archipelagoes,
From points of land moved by wind and water
Out of where they used to be to where they are,
The people of the earth marched and travelled
To gather on a great plain.

by Carl Sandburg from *The People, Yes.*

1

The Scandinavian Heritage

From the four corners of the earth,
from corners lashed in wind
and bitten with rain and fire
from places where the winds begin
and fogs are born with mist children,
tall men from tall rocky slopes came
and sleepy men from sleepy valleys,
their women tall, their women sleepy,
with bundles and belongings,
with little ones babbling, "Where to now?
what next?"

by Carl Sandburg from *The People, Yes.*

The first European child born on the North American continent may well have been a Scandinavian. The sagas of the Vikings—ancestors of the Scandinavians—record the birth of an infant boy named Snorri, during the winter of 1003-1004 A.D. Snorri first saw the light of day, we are told, in a land the Vikings called Vinland, meaning Wineland. This land, reportedly discovered a few years earlier by Leif Ericson, was rich and plentiful. There the Vikings had found fish and game in abundance, along with good grazing for their cattle, wild rice (which they called "self-sown wheat"), and grapes, from which came the land's name.

Snorri, along with 60 men, five women, and various livestock, made up the colony, which stayed in Vinland for only a year or two. In 1006, the sagas report, after battles with some of the "dark-skinned" native inhabitants of the land, the would-be colonists returned to the thriving Viking colonies in Greenland.

Historians sharply disagree on where Vinland was located. But most think that it lay somewhere south of Greenland, on the coast of Labrador or Nova Scotia, or perhaps farther south, in New England, or even on the banks of the Hudson River in New York.

Though the colony did not survive, many Scandinavians recall its history proudly. While all Americans celebrate Christopher Columbus Day on October 12, many Scandinavian-Americans also celebrate Leif Ericson Day on October 9, honoring the discoverer of Vinland.

Other Viking colonies *did* survive. Viking colonists were living in Greenland at least until the 14th century; some of their descendants may still have been living there when Christopher Columbus began his famous explorations across the mid-Atlantic in 1492. But there were not, as far as we know, any continuing Viking settlements in North America itself.

Modern Immigration

When Northern Europeans once again began to colonize the mainland—more successfully this time—Scandinavians were among the earliest settlers. Swedes and Finns arrived in the Delaware Bay area and settled in Pennsylvania in 1638, over 40 years before William Penn. Danes and Norwegians came with the Dutch to colonies such as New Amsterdam (now New York) in the same period. Other Scandinavians, mostly sailors, occasionally came and stayed in America in the next two centuries.

However, the main Scandinavian immigration began in the 19th century, peaking in the 1880s and continuing until the worldwide Depression of the 1930s. Danes and Norwegians started with modest migrations in the early decades of the 19th century, then began to send large numbers after the 1850s, as early pioneers were opening the Midwest. Swedes, more tightly restricted by their government, were only free to travel from the 1840s on. For all three groups, migration continued to be heavy throughout the 19th century, as Scandinavians helped to open and settle the American West.

Being more isolated, both the Finns and Icelanders started emigrating (leaving their homelands) somewhat later. The Finns began heavy emigration in the 1860s, peaking only in the first two decades of the 20th century, and the Icelanders left largely between the 1870s and 1900.

Emigration from most parts of Scandinavia, as from all Northern Europe, began to tail off somewhat in the early 20th century. Then, in the 1920s, the United States set up quotas, limiting the number of immigrants it would accept from each country. Swedish and Icelandic immigration had by then fallen off enough so that the quotas set for their countries had little practical effect. But the flow of Finns, Norwegians, and Danes was still in excess of the new quotas, and was diverted instead to other countries, such as Canada. Finally, with the Great Depression of the 1930s, Scandinavian immigration dropped off almost to nothing. Indeed, in those hard times, many Scandinavian immigrants left the United States to return home.

Some small numbers of Scandinavian immigrants have come to the United States since World War II. But in recent years, just as before the 19th century, some of the Scandinavian countries—especially Sweden— have been attractive enough to potential immigrants that fewer of their citizens have left for the United States.

This book is about the whole immigration to the United States from the Scandinavian countries; about the Scandinavian people themselves; about why and how they came; and about how they helped to shape the new land they adopted as their own. To understand the Scandinavians' contributions to America, we must understand the heritage they brought with them to the new land.

The Heritage

By any standards, the Scandinavians—the Danes, the Finns, the Icelanders, the Norwegians, and the Swedes—are a remarkable people. Their explorations and settlements in the North Atlantic lands were just one part of their extraordinary background. In the early Middle Ages, especially from the seventh to the tenth centuries, the Vikings streamed out of their northern homelands in all directions. Before they were through, they had conquered and settled lands from the Arctic Circle to North Africa, and from America to the heart of Russia.

The sagas, the great heroic stories of Vikings, record the glory of those times, much as Homer's *Iliad* and *Odyssey* recorded the exploits of the early Greeks. These sagas kept alive the Viking heritage. Because sagas were retold from generation to generation, the Scandinavians brought to America a love of literature. Their religion also contributed to that love.

After the 17th century, everyone in Scandinavia was required to become confirmed in the Lutheran Church—and to do that, they had to learn how to read. So Scandinavians have traditionally had a very high literacy rate.

The result was that Scandinavians were better able than many other ethnic groups to take advantage of what America had to offer. Knowing how to read and write in their own language, they were able to more easily learn English, a language closely related to the Scandinavian languages. In America, which guaranteed freedom of the press from the 1780s on, the whole world of learning and education was open to them. So they could and did easily move into the professional fields—education, science, engineering, medicine, law, politics, and the like. In this way Scandinavian immigrants and their descendants had a very great influence on the shape of America, to some small extent in the early years and to a very great extent in the 19th and 20th centuries.

The Scandinavians historically have also had strong religious views. The overwhelming majority of them, both at home and in America, were Lutherans. However, they often disagreed on the form the Lutheran Church should take, especially in America. A large number of Scandinavian immigrants even disagreed with the Lutheran Church altogether and came to America as dissenters. They were Mormons, Quakers, Baptists, Methodists, and other kinds of Protestants, seeking freedom to worship in their own way. Religion was an important part of life for them, in both the old country and the new. It still is. Among the strongly religious, often fundamentalist, believers who today form the backbone of mid-America, many are of Scandinavian descent.

The Scandinavians have also traditionally had a strong feeling for freedom and equality. Many of the Vikings who streamed out across the world in the Middle Ages did so to avoid submitting to an unwanted king. They wanted the independence to rule themselves as they wished. Scandinavians may often have found themselves as unwilling subjects—at various times, Norway, Denmark, or Sweden has been dominant over other Scandinavian peoples—but they still have a strong tradition of democracy. Iceland, in fact, has the world's oldest continuing parliament, the Althing, founded in 930.

America may owe the Vikings an even greater debt. The American concepts of freedom and equality—the ideas and practices that make America unique in all the world—draw partly on Viking traditions, brought to New England by the early British settlers. Many of the British are themselves of Scandinavian stock, for the Vikings had overrun and colonized much of the British Isles during the Middle Ages.

With their feeling for freedom and equality, the Scandinavians also had strong traditions of mutual aid and cooperation. Like many of the early New England settlers, some tried to establish first in Scandinavia and later in America, utopian societies—often small communities that shared property and power equally among their members. Few of these idealistic societies lasted very long, though the ideas continued to thrive. But many other Scandinavian immigrants brought with them practical experience of cooperative movements in their homelands, which had more longlasting influence. The American cooperatives of the late 19th and early 20th century, which were such a boon to farmers, were very much modeled on their Scandinavian counterparts. With industrialization in the 19th century, many Scandinavians, in both the old country and the new, fought for the rights of working people, for fair pay, reasonable hours, and safe working conditions.

The Scandinavians also brought with them to America an enormous capacity for hard work. Dominated by mountains and water, Scandinavia

In his poetry, Swedish-American Carl Sandburg spoke of all the skills, intelligence, strength, endurance, and vitality that immigrants brought to America. (Library of Congress)

(except for Denmark) is mostly "hardscrabble" land, where much labor brings little reward. To survive there, Scandinavians had to be tough people not afraid to work. And the opening of the new lands of North America called for just that kind of people. The farmlands of North America are rich now—as rich as any in the world. But they came into being only because settlers were determined enough to clear and plow the land, hardy enough to bear extremes of temperature unknown in their homelands, and intelligent enough to learn a whole new way of life in a frontier land. Much of the heartland of mid-America—breadbasket of the nation and, to some extent, the world—was first brought under the plow by Scandinavian-Americans.

Scandinavians brought many skills with them to the new land. Because farming was so difficult in much of Scandinavia, these people for centuries had made all or part of their living in other ways. Some drew on the bountiful sea, working as sailors, trading across the seas, and fishing—for their own food and for sale to others. In America, they employed many of these same skills, notably along the New England coast, on the Great Lakes, and along the Pacific coast from California to Alaska.

Others drew on the skills they had learned in the forests of Scandinavia. They worked as loggers, made such by-products as tar from trees, and did fine woodwork, both at home during the long, dark winters and later in factories. These skills were much appreciated in America, especially in the forested lands all along the Canadian border.

Some things that are now considered a part of "American" life were originally Scandinavian. The log cabin that has been a fixture of America's pioneer image from the 17th century was of Swedish design. Scandinavians, especially Norwegians, introduced skiing to America. More recently, the Finns gave us the *sauna*, the heated bathhouse so common in today's health clubs.

More than all that, the Scandinavians contributed much to the "image" of America. The traditional picture of the "all-American" boy and girl—tall, lean, fair-haired, fair-skinned, light-eyed, athletic, looking like they just stepped off a Midwestern farm—owes more than a little to the many Scandinavian settlers of the Midwest.

Indeed, if the United States is seen as a great tapestry, it is the Scandinavians who joined with the British and other Northern European Protestants to form the underlying fabric of the land. On this ground, they and other ethnic groups wove many colorful strands of history and formed them into the fascinating and varied picture that is America today.

2

The Children of the Vikings

Scandinavia is a land of oceans, lakes, and rivers; of stunningly beautiful *fjords*, the long, narrow inlets that push inland from the seas; of forests, which supply lumber for building and handcrafts; of farms, often small holdings won with great difficulty from the surrounding woodlands; of rocky coasts and sheltered islands.

The great, wooded, craggy peninsula shared by Sweden and Norway hangs down like a huge bunch of grapes from the "stem" of Finland, which backs on Russia to the east. Pointing northward toward that large peninsula is the flatter, smaller, more hospitable, and more heavily settled peninsula of Denmark, jutting out from Germany. These Scandinavian lands, along with Germany, almost surround Europe's island-dotted Baltic Sea.

Sweden, on the eastern side of the great Scandinavian peninsula, faces the Baltic Sea, gateway to the East through the many rivers of Russia. On the west side of the peninsula, Norway faces the North Sea and beyond it the British Isles and the whole North Atlantic Ocean. To the north, above the Arctic Circle, lies the icy Barents Sea. Denmark and Finland, too, are lands dominated by water.

It is no wonder then that Scandinavians, many of whom have traditionally made all or part of their living from fishing, headed out across the seas. Some who did so in the early Middle Ages made a "little Scandinavia" in Iceland, over 600 miles out in the North Atlantic and partway between Europe and North America. This far outpost of Scandinavia is a witness to the great days of the Viking peoples.

Beautiful though these lands are, they have never been heavily populated. In 1815, for example, Sweden had only 2,500,000 people,

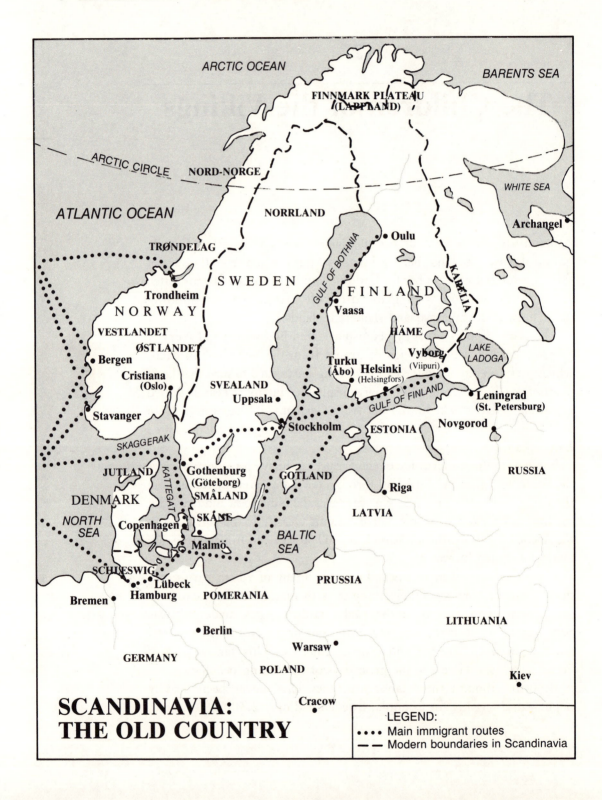

ARCTIC OCEAN

BARENTS SEA

FINNMARK PLATEAU
(LAPPLAND)

ARCTIC CIRCLE

NORD-NORGE

WHITE SEA

ATLANTIC OCEAN

NORRLAND

Archangel

TRØNDELAG

Oulu

GULF OF BOTHNIA

SWEDEN

FINLAND

KARELIA

Trondheim

Vaasa

NORWAY

VESTLANDET

ØSTLANDET

HÄME

LAKE
LADOGA

Bergen

Vyborg
(Viipuri)

Cristiana
(Oslo)

Turku
(Åbo)

Helsinki
(Helsingfors)

SVEALAND

Uppsala

Leningrad
(St. Petersburg)

Stavanger

Stockholm

ESTONIA

Novgorod

SKAGGERAK

GULF OF FINLAND

RUSSIA

JUTLAND

KATTEGAT

Gothenburg
(Göteborg)

GOTLAND

Riga

DENMARK

SMÅLAND

LATVIA

NORTH
SEA

Copenhagen

SKÅNE

Malmö

BALTIC
SEA

SCHLESWIG

PRUSSIA

Lübeck

Bremen

Hamburg

POMERANIA

LITHUANIA

Berlin

GERMANY

Warsaw

POLAND

Kiev

**SCANDINAVIA:
THE OLD COUNTRY**

Cracow

LEGEND:
•••• Main immigrant routes
‒ ‒ ‒ Modern boundaries in Scandinavia

though the population has more than tripled since then. Norway had fewer than 900,000, Finland perhaps 1,500,000, and Iceland only a few tens of thousands. Even Denmark, small but more heavily settled, had under 2,000,000 people in that period. The lands of Scandinavia cover territory about three times the size of California and 10 times the size of England. But even today, after nearly two centuries of rapid growth, they have altogether a population of only 22 million.

The reasons for this small population are not hard to find. Except for Denmark, most of which is rich farming land, Scandinavia is rough country. Even after land has been cleared with great labor, it has poor soil for farming. Heavy forests cover much of the land. Being so far north, the land is hidden in almost total darkness for part of the winter, with deep frost and longlasting snow. In the summer, the reverse is true; in May and June, the day lasts for 23 to 24 hours. But beautiful though these summer months are, the short growing season still means a hard life for small farmers. They might not be able to farm the land at all except that the Gulf Stream—that great, warm river in the Atlantic Ocean—passes near both Iceland and the northwestern part of the Scandinavian Peninsula, somewhat moderating the harsh temperatures. Because of this, farming in Scandinavia is carried on farther north than in anywhere else in the world.

The Scandinavian Peoples

Like all the peoples of the Earth, the Scandinavians—Swedes, Norwegians, Danes, Finns, and Icelanders—are of mixed background. They are descendants of the many waves of peoples who have swept across Europe during the tens of thousands of years of human history.

The largest part of the Scandinavian heritage comes from the Indo-European-speaking peoples, who began to move into Western Europe from southern Russia over 5,000 years ago. The descendants of these Indo-Europeans today dominate most of Europe and much of Western Asia, from Scotland to India, from Spain to Russia. Swedes, Danes, Norwegians, and their descendants the Icelanders trace much of their ancestry to the Germanic branch of the Indo-Europeans, as do some Finns.

Other peoples of different backgrounds once held the lands of Scandinavia, and some of their descendants still live there. By at least 8,000 years ago, the Lapps or Laplanders—a rather short, dark-haired people—had occupied Scandinavia. For thousands of years they roamed the region, hunting and fishing on the seashores and lakes, in the forests and mountains. At some later point—we do not really know quite when or from where—Finns began to move into the region, pushing the Laplanders away from the prime shorelands into less attractive lands, mostly to the north.

Then, 4,000 to 5,000 years ago, waves of newer migrants, mostly Indo-Europeans, came to the attractive shores of Scandinavia. They brought with them such innovations as agriculture and domesticated animals, like the horse. They did not penetrate far inland, however. At around the time of Christ, 2,000 years ago, Finnish-speaking peoples still held much of Scandinavia. The background of the Finns is complex and unclear, and we know very little about just who they were. Certainly their language is quite different from the Indo-European family of languages.

In the coming centuries, the Finns—who had earlier pushed Laplanders to the north—were themselves pushed farther away from the southern shores by newer immigrants: the Germanic wing of the Indo-European peoples. It would be some centuries before the Germanic peoples would penetrate the frozen, less hospitable lands to the north and east. During that time, the Lapps and the Finns to some extent kept their old language and culture—as many of them still do today. Those who remained along the shore gradually merged with the newcomers, losing any distinct cultural identity.

The descendants of these various waves of immigrants form the Scandinavian peoples we know today. Physically, the Scandinavians (apart from the Laplanders) are much alike, generally tall and rather lean, often fair-haired, fair-skinned, and blue- or gray-eyed. Over the years, they have gradually diverged in both language and culture.

But whatever the differences that have emerged, the Scandinavians remain closely allied with each other, not only in background but also in language and culture. Though their pronunciation and writing differ somewhat, Norwegians, Swedes, and Danes can understand each other's languages quite readily. The Icelandic language has changed less over the centuries and is more like Old Norse. Only Finnish differs markedly.

The histories of these Scandinavian peoples have, for centuries, been intertwined. Like members of a great family, they have often battled among themselves. But they also share the common heritage of the great Viking Age.

On their distant voyages, Vikings often converted their ships into temporary, tent-covered shelters while ashore.
(Author's archives)

The Viking Heritage

For reasons not entirely clear, the largest Scandinavian groups—the Norwegians, the Danes, and the Swedes—began to expand in all directions from their northern homelands, starting in about 800 A.D. While the Swedes looked toward the east, toward Finland and Russia, the Norwegians and Danes looked to the west, and later to the whole North Atlantic.

From about 800 to 1050 A.D., the Scandinavians dominated much of Europe. They were then generally known as "Vikings," a word that means "raiders." The term is apt, because these Vikings built an empire on raiding, before they settled down to trading. For a time during these centuries, Vikings had almost encircled Europe, and they wandered freely in the North Atlantic.

Vikings from the area of modern Sweden generally headed eastward across the Baltic Sea and the Gulf of Finland into Russia. They were also called *Rus*—we know them as the Russians. And the empire they founded was named after them—Russia. Heading down the Russian rivers, the Rus established a major trading empire, with centers at Novgorod, near Lake Ladoga and just east of the Gulf of Finland, and Kiev, farther south and along the Dnieper River. Their influence reached all the way south to

Constantinople, the capital of the Byzantine Empire, to which Viking traders would make annual trading voyages carrying furs and other desirable items. They became so rich and powerful that the Rurik dynasty they founded in Russia lasted until the 1600s, when the Romanov dynasty took power. They also became Christians in the late 10th century, adopting the Eastern Orthodox form of the religion, which was based in Constantinople.

Meanwhile those Vikings who had stayed in their Swedish homeland adopted the Roman Catholic form of Christianity in the ninth century. By the 11th and 12th centuries, both the Swedes and the Russians were trying to dominate Finland. The rivalry was, for a time, expressed largely in religious terms, as each tried to convert the Finns to their own form of Christianity.

Swedish missionaries made many converts in southwestern Finland in the 11th century. In 1155, the Swedish King Eric followed up these missions with a crusade to Finland. A second Swedish crusade nearly a century later penetrated into the lake district of Häme. By the end of the 13th century, the Swedes had taken their religion all the way into the eastern province of Karelia, marking their progress by building a great castle at Vyborg (in Finnish, Viipuri) in 1293.

There the Swedes met the Russians, who were still attempting to convert the Finns to the Eastern Orthodox religion. The Russians, in any case, regarded Karelia as theirs. In 1323, the two countries divided the district of Karelia between them, setting the first—but far from the last—formal eastern boundary for Finland.

As they traveled the rivers of Europe, Viking traders often hauled their boats overland from one waterway to the next.
(Det Kongelige Bibliotek, Copenhagen)

The West Vikings

Meanwhile, Norwegian and Danish Vikings had turned primarily to the west. They raided and then settled many of the islands, seacoasts, and riverbanks of northwestern Europe. Norwegian Vikings focused first on Scotland and Ireland, as well as the Atlantic Islands north and west of the British Isles, such as the Shetlands, the Orkneys, and the Hebrides.

The Danes spread first to the lowlands of Europe, especially to the Dutch and French coasts. Then, starting in the eighth century, Danish Vikings crossed the English Channel and took large parts of the British Isles. Some people feel that these fiercely independent Danish Vikings gave the English people one of their greatest treasures: a feeling for equality, a desire to rule themselves as equals, rather than to be subordinated to an all-powerful king. This later bore fruit not only in England but also in the new land of America.

Denmark was a power to be reckoned with in this period. Harold Bluetooth, who ruled in the 10th century, proclaimed that he had "won all Denmark and Norway and made the Danes Christians." In this period Denmark also included parts of southern Sweden, notably the coastal plains of Skåne. For a brief period in the 11th century, King Canute II of Denmark ruled much of Norway and England as well.

Danish Vikings also took large parts of France, including Normandy, which is named after these "Northmen." Their descendants, known as Normans, later invaded England from France in 1066, changing England's history forever. Some Danish Vikings also followed the European coast southward, sometimes slicing cross-country through river valleys, to southern France and Italy. Others later moved farther east, to the Byzantine Empire, completing the Viking circle around Europe.

The Atlantic Vikings

Meanwhile, the Norwegian Vikings had generally headed westward across the Atlantic, from their settlements in both Norway and the British Isles. Hopping from island to island—from the Shetlands, the Orkneys, the Hebrides, and the Faeroes, to Iceland and Greenland—they made their way to North America, and the unidentified Vinland.

They may well have traveled north through the icy straits to Hudson's

Bay or far down the east coast of North America. A Viking settlement on the northeast coast of Newfoundland, at L'Anse Aux Meadows, was discovered by archaeologists in 1960. Surprisingly, out of eight huts in the settlement, three have iron-working furnaces. It seems likely that this was a ship repair site where blacksmiths worked to refit Viking ships for long voyages.

Norwegian Vikings wanted to be free and independent of their homeland. Harold I (The Fairhaired) had unified Norway in 872 A.D. But some Norwegian adventurers broke away from that union and headed across the Atlantic in about 874 A.D. The Norwegian Vikings remained independent in Iceland and Greenland for almost four centuries. There they prospered, farming, fishing, and trading with Europe. Their main export was homespun cloth, largely wool.

Through trading ships, these Atlantic Vikings kept up some ties with their homeland. Christianity had been introduced to Norway in the 10th century and made the official religion in the 11th. Iceland and the other Atlantic settlements adopted Christianity in the year 1000. After that both Greenland and Iceland were sent bishops, who reported periodically to the Norwegian archbishop in Trondheim, Viking seat on the Atlantic coast of Norway.

But the independence of the Atlantic Vikings did not last. By the 1260s, they were obliged to swear loyalty to the Norwegian king. For centuries after that they sent yearly tribute to the king at Trondheim.

The weather also turned against them. As the Atlantic world grew colder—in the "Little Ice Age" of the 12th to the 16th centuries—Vikings were gradually forced to withdraw from their westernmost settlements. The last of Eric the Red's descendants in Greenland may have survived there into the century when Christopher Columbus was born. But by the late 15th or early 16th century, what few settlers had remained in these western Atlantic outposts had retreated to Iceland.

Unions and Divisions

In the Norwegian and Danish homelands, civil wars were frequent. The rulers of Denmark often battled German princes over fertile lands such as those of Schleswig and Holstein, on the southern part of the Danish peninsula. Strong rulers might unite the region temporarily, but the union would fracture again.

All Scandinavia was weakened by the Black Death, the plague that killed perhaps one-quarter to one-third of Europe's population. By the late 14th century, Norway was so much weakened that its ships no longer sailed westward. What little contact Norwegians still had with peoples in the Atlantic was carried on in the ships of other nations. As a result, the thrones of Norway and Denmark were united. The two were joined in 1397 by Sweden (which included Finland) in the Union of Kalmar.

As Denmark entered its age of empire, Norway slid under its rule. It was officially named a province in 1537 and remained so until 1814. Iceland, after becoming a colony of Norway, gradually passed into the hands of Denmark, as did most of the other Atlantic territories settled by the Vikings. These were the centuries of the great Northern European trading network called the Hanseatic League, in which all the Scandinavian countries played a part—and Denmark played a central role.

However, Sweden was unhappy with the Union of Kalmar. In 1523 anti-union forces united under Gustav Vasa and pulled Sweden out of the union. Gustav was elected king of Sweden, founding the Vasa dynasty. Then Sweden embarked on its own course of empire-building.

By this period, on the brink of the modern age, the Scandinavians had settled gradually into the lands in which we find them today. And, more than most people, the history of the Scandinavians was to be shaped by the lands in which they live.

The Swedish Background

Of all the Scandinavian countries, Sweden is the largest. It stretches for almost 1,000 miles from north to south, about the distance between Chicago and New York. It is no wonder that the Swedish call their country "our long-drawn-out land." The northern half of the country is the iron-rich, fir-covered region called Norrland. Here lumbering and mining for metals are the main occupations of a small population. The Swedes did not colonize this area until about 1000 A.D., leaving it primarily to the Lapps.

The heart of Sweden is the eastern-central lowlands region called Svealand, after one of the early Swedish tribes, the Svear. This is a land of many lakes, fertile plains, and small towns. Here the pines and spruces of the north are joined by birches and aspens. The coast of Svealand is rocky, dotted with hundreds of small islands. The national capital, Stockholm, is built across so many islands that it is sometimes called "The Venice of the North." The ancient city of Uppsala—a university town and center of the Lutheran church in Sweden—is also located on the coast of Svealand. The people here have generally supplemented their farming, lumbering, or mining with fishing and trading.

The southernmost region of Sweden is Goteland, named for another early Swedish tribe, the Gotar. Ninety percent of Sweden's people today live in Svealand and Goteland. And it was these two regions that sent most of the country's immigrants to America.

Goteland is itself divided into two portions: the piney highlands called Småland and, on the southern rim, and area of rich plains called Skåne. Småland has stony soil and only small-scale agriculture and industry, mostly in forest products. About one-third of all Swedish immigrants to the United States came from Småland.

Skåne is the most heavily populated part of Sweden. The two main cities in Skåne are Gothenburg (Göteborg), the main western seaport through which most of Sweden's emigration flowed, and Malmö, only a few miles across the water from Copenhagen, Denmark. These westward-facing ports remain open throughout the winter, unlike the Baltic ports, which are likely to be frozen for several months a year.

The 17th century was Sweden's "Age of Greatness," largely created by Gustav Vasa's grandson, Gustavus Adolphus, who ruled from 1611 to 1632. The empire he created included Finland and other eastern and southern coastal regions of the Baltic Sea.

Under the 17th-century reign of King Gustavus Adolphus, Sweden became a major Protestant nation.
(Library of Congress)

Under Gustavus Adolphus, Sweden broke with the Roman Catholic Church and became a strong Lutheran state, holding the balance of power in Europe. Some called Gustavus Adolphus the "Savior of Protestantism," for his leadership in Europe's Catholic-Protestant conflicts, called the Thirty Years' War. During this period, many persecuted Protestants found refuge in Sweden. In 1660, Sweden and Denmark, old rivals, settled their boundaries, with Skåne going to Sweden. Sweden's battles with Russia continued on and off until 1809, when Finland was surrendered to Russia.

In that same year, after a period of strict repression, Sweden bloodlessly deposed the last Vasa monarch. From then until 1905, Sweden was the stronger partner in the Norway-Sweden union. In the 19th century a number of liberalizing reforms, and also industrialization, established the foundation for the modern Swedish state. From 1814 on, Sweden has been at peace with the world.

The Norwegian Background

The country of Norway—the name means "The Northern Way"—is even more "long-drawn-out" than Sweden. To some, Norway looks like a fish, with the "head" pointing south toward Denmark and Germany, and the narrower "fishtail" flapping in the Arctic Ocean. Almost 1,600 miles long, Norway lies on the western side of the mountainous spine of the Scandinavian Peninsula. But in the Arctic regions, where the "fishtail" curves around Sweden to meet Finland and Russia, Norway is in some places barely four miles wide.

Norway is a hard land, dominated by mountains, lakes, and glaciers. Only 3 to 4 percent of the land can be farmed, so the population, always small, supplements farming with logging and fishing. As one Norwegian put it: "What would we be without the sea? A handful of people on a pile of rocks!" Only in the last century have Norwegians been able to build some prosperity from mining and hydroelectric power, and, of course, shipping.

Southern Norway is divided by mountains into two parts: Østlandet (Eastern Norway) and Vestlandet (Western Norway). Over half of Norway's population lives in Østlandet, many of them in the nation's capital of Oslo, called Christiana or Kristiana between 1624 and 1925. In these temperate lands near Sweden lie many small farms, lumbering communities, and vacation resorts, as well as much of the country's industry.

The craggy coastline of Vestlandet, facing the Atlantic Ocean, is quite different. It is marked by many deep fjords—long, narrow, winding, glacier-gouged inlets, like so many gnarled fingers poking into Norway from the North Sea and the Atlantic Ocean. Because of the shelter these fjords provide and the relatively warm climate brought by the Gulf Stream, Vestlandet is noted for its agricultural products, especially its fruits. Second to farming, quite naturally, are fishing and trading. The Vestlandet city of Bergen was, during the great days of Northern European trade, a major port. Many early Norwegian emigrants left from Vestlandet's southerly ports, such as Stavanger, facing toward Britain.

In central Norway lies the attractive region of Trøndelag, centered around the city of Trondheim, second largest city of Norway and capital of the country during the great Viking Age. Trondheim lies at the head of the great, unusually wide Trondheimsfjord. Farming and lumbering dominate here, too, along with mining. Like Østlandet, which it much resembles, Trøndelag has widespread spruce woods, leafy birches, ashes, rowans, and aspens, and under it all a thick carpet of mosses and heather.

The fjord country of Scandinavia has breathtaking scenery, such as this 1,800-foot drop to the water, at Pulpit Rock near Stavanger.
(Photo by Norwegian National Tourist Office, Library of Congress)

This Norwegian home of the late 19th century uses a fitted log construction, cousin to the log cabin design early Scandinavians brought to 17th-century America.
(Library of Congress)

North of Trøndelag and most above the Arctic Circle lies Nord-Norge, the famous "Land of the Midnight Sun," where the population lives in total darkness for two months in the winter, but in total daylight two months of the summer. Here, few trees are found, apart from pines in inland valleys. Fishing is the main occupation. But in modern times, Nord-Norge has also seen some mining and industry.

In the far north, especially in the Finnmark Plateau adjoining Finland, live many Laplanders, descendants of much earlier inhabitants of Scandinavia. In the 19th century, many Finns immigrated to Nord-Norge, generally to work in the mines there. Some of these immigrants were later recruited to work in United States mines.

From 1397 until the end of the Napoleonic Wars, Norway was little more than a poor cousin in a family ruled by Denmark. Then, in 1814, Denmark, which had been allied with the defeated Napoleon, was forced to give Norway to Sweden. Though Norway tried to break free, Sweden enforced the Act of Union of 1815, creating an unequal dual kingdom of Norway and Sweden, with Norway still the poor cousin. This union lasted until 1905, when it was dissolved peacefully, and the Norwegians elected their own king by popular referendum.

The Finnish Background

Finland, in territory the second largest of the Scandinavian countries, is also a land that stretches mainly from north to south. In the north it touches on Sweden, Norway, and Russia, which also forms its entire eastern border. The land itself lies nestled in an L-shaped berth between two long arms of the Baltic Sea, the gulfs of Bothnia and Finland.

The Gulf of Finland runs south of Finland to the Russian city of Leningrad (formerly St. Petersburg), at one time Finnish territory. Historically this was one of the main Viking routes into Russia. And, in the reverse direction, many invaders have come toward Finland on this route over the centuries. Finland's border with Russia to the east has long been a matter of dispute.

The largest city in Finland, Helsinki (in Swedish, Helsingfors), lies on the Gulf of Finland. The capital, Turku (in Swedish Åbo), also lies on Finland's southern coast, facing the Baltic Sea. For centuries, Finland was centered on the many small shipbuilding ports facing the Gulf of Bothnia. Then in the 19th century, Bothnia's lumbering, tarmaking, and shipbuilding centers declined. So the majority of Finland's immigrants to America came from these Bothnian coastal provinces, especially from around the ports of Vaasa and Oulu.

Finland is much colder than Norway and Sweden. With more low hills than lofty mountains, it is also more heavily forested with pine, spruce, and birches. Lakes and bogs cover over 10 percent of the country—50 percent in part of the north. The small, poor, and isolated farms that dot the land look from the air like islands in a stream. Today the great rivers draining these lakes provide much of Finland's hydroelectric power.

Finland is divided into three main regions. First is the coastal plain facing the sea. Here are found many farms and most of the principal cities of Finland. This area was settled by a group of Finns known as the Suomalaiset. These settlers gave their name to the whole country, which is known to the Finns themselves as Suomi, or Suomen Tasavalta.

Inland is the great lake district of Häme that gives Finland the nickname, "The Land of the Thousand Lakes." Long rather isolated, some parts of this lake district have only recently become industrialized, and are popular with summer vacationers. This region is named after an early group of Finnish settlers, the Hämäläiset.

The far north of Finland, on somewhat higher, but still boggy land, is a lightly populated area. Stunted forests gradually give way to frozen, treeless tundra. Here the inhabitants, many of them Lapps, lead a seminomadic life by following their herds of reindeer, though they also do some small dairy farming.

To the east of present-day Finland is a province called Karelia, after the Finnish group that settled there, the Karelians. This province is now a part of the Soviet Union, but has been a part of Finland in centuries past.

The Finns have had few periods of independence during their modern history. Between the 12th and 19th centuries, Sweden sent many colonists to Finland, primarily to the coastal regions. During Sweden's imperial era, Finland's border was pushed all the way east to Lake Ladoga, once Viking territory. This was well east of where the city of St. Petersburg (today, Russia's great western port of Leningrad) would be built a century later. In that period, the Swedes—and therefore also the Finns—broke with the Roman Catholic Church and became Protestant.

Caught in a series of Swedish wars during the 17th and 18th centuries, Finland was drained of men and resources. In the late 17th century, the country also suffered a severe famine, which may have killed as much as one-third of the nation's population. More and more Finnish territory was lost to the Russians. At one point in the early 18th century, Russia occupied Finland and devastated it; the period is known as the Great Wrath.

Finally, in 1809, the Swedes were forced to give Finland to Russia. The country then became a grand duchy of the czar. Only after the Russian Revolution of 1917 was Finland able to proclaim its independence. That was recognized by its new Communist neighbor in 1920. Even so, the province of Karelia was lost to the Soviet Union after World War II.

During the long years of Swedish control, Swedish colonists gathered more and more power in Finland. These Swedish-speaking Finns, or Swede-Finns, were less than 10 percent of the population, but they long dominated Finland socially, politically, and economically. As a result many strains arose between Finnish-speakers and Swedish-speakers over the centuries, although Finland today is officially bilingual.

The Danish Background

Denmark is something of a bridge between Scandinavia and the rest of Europe. It consists of a small peninsula called Jutland, only 42 miles wide at the neck, jutting out into the North Sea from Germany, and nearly 500 islands, reaching almost to Sweden and Norway. It has been a crossroads of Europe for thousands of years, the pathway taken by most of the early invaders of Scandinavia, first by nomadic hunters, later farmers, and then Christian missionaries.

Surrounded by water, Denmark also dominates the sea-lanes between the Baltic Sea and the North Sea, and beyond that, the Atlantic. The narrow straits between Denmark and Sweden—Kattegat to the east and Skagerrak to the north—have been the prime routes for Scandinavian sailors and traders throughout history. They were the key to Denmark's dominance during the Middle Ages. And they are the reason behind the rise of Denmark's capital and main port, Copenhagen (København), on an island just a ferryboat ride away from Malmö, Sweden. Through these straits many America-bound Swedes, Finns, and Danes traveled until the mid-19th century, when railroads were built allowing shortcuts overland to ports more directly facing the Atlantic.

Quite unlike other Scandinavian countries, Denmark is not dominated by mountains. Apart from the sandy dunes of Jutland, its predominant lowlands are nearly all excellent farmland, traditionally planted with cereal grains or roots such as potatoes or beets. In the past two centuries, Danish farmers have turned increasingly to dairy and poultry farming. Because it is such fertile land, Denmark is far more heavily settled than other parts of Scandinavia.

Denmark today is only a small part of what it once was. Danes once ruled Norway, Iceland, and large parts of Sweden and the British Isles, as well as some territory that is now considered part of Germany. Until 1953, Greenland was a Danish colony. For a time Denmark even had a toehold in the Caribbean; it was known then as the Danish West Indies, but today as the Virgin Islands. Over the centuries when Europeans were gradually settling America, Denmark declined from a great empire to the small, strongly independent country it is now.

The Icelandic Background

Iceland is a land of fire and ice, a land of active volcanoes and hot geysers set amid icy glaciers. On the edge of the Arctic Circle, it lies far out in the Atlantic, some 180 miles southeast of Greenland and over 600 miles west of Norway. In many ways it is much like southern Norway, a land dominated by the ocean, full of fjords and bays

It is not quite as cold as its name implies for, like parts of Scandinavia, it is warmed by the Atlantic's Gulf Stream. But Iceland is far from a bountiful land. This great mass of volcanic rock is almost treeless and has poor vegetation in most areas. Only about one-sixth of the land can be farmed. Most of Iceland's small population is concentrated in the coastal lowlands of the south and west.

Icelanders have proud traditions, however. In this oceanbound land, the early Vikings established an independent republic, with their famous parliament, the Althing. Icelanders trace their ancestry directly back to the Vikings. One work, the *Landnámabók (Book of Settlements)*, even lists some 400 of the earliest Viking immigrants, detailing where they came from and where they settled. In addition to these Vikings, Celtic peoples from Ireland and Scotland also joined the settlement in Iceland. Many were probably of mixed Celtic and Scandinavian ancestry, since they came from some of the coastal regions the Vikings had conquered earlier.

A large number of the Celtic immigrants in the Middle Ages were religious hermits, who sometimes took off from the British Isles in tiny boats to settle on Atlantic islands. Indeed, some of them probably arrived in Iceland before 800 A.D. and were there when the first Vikings arrived in the 870s. These monks had little success either in converting the Vikings to Christianity, or in much influencing Icelandic culture. After this early period, few additional immigrants came to Iceland.

In the early days of the Viking expansion, Iceland was a trading hub, exporting homespun cloth to other parts of the Atlantic and keeping in regular contact with Norway. But by the 12th century, the climate was growing colder, and life grew harder. As this "Little Ice Age" descended, people gradually abandoned the westernmost Atlantic outposts in Greenland, retreating to Iceland.

In this period Iceland itself underwent a dramatic change, as farming became more difficult. Where most Icelanders had made their living raising sheep and other animals, they now made fishing their main occupation. The textile trade virtually disappeared, and Iceland's main exports became dried fish and fish oil.

But hard times hit Scandinavia, too. The fleet that had once plied the waters between Iceland and Northern Europe fell into decay. Lacking the wood to build their own fleet, Icelanders had to rely on others to ship their goods. During the 15th century, ships from England and from Northern

Europe's Hanseatic League traded with Iceland. Then in 1602 Denmark decided to close down Iceland altogether to outside contacts. Iceland became totally dependent on the whims of Denmark.

Modern Times

The Vikings of old had had a strong tradition of independence and equality. But in later centuries, when Scandinavians became empire-builders of a different sort, the government was far from democratic. A relatively small group of aristocrats held power. Although monarchs were elected, only people of some property and position could vote. The vast majority of the population had no say in the government of the country.

The centuries of America's youth were also centuries of major change in Scandinavia. Population was rising sharply and industry was growing; both factors caused many disruptions in once-quiet lives, while an oversupply of rural laborers were flooding to the cities looking for work. The stage was set for the massive migration from Scandinavia to America.

3

Breathing Free

Here [in America] at last I can breathe freely. Here no one is persecuted for his religious convictions. Each person can worship God in any way that agrees with his persuasion. Pickpockets and lawyers, unscrupulous debt collectors, morally corrupted officials and idlers are here deprived of all power to harm the people. No barriers stand in the way of free enterprise. Everyone enjoys undisturbed the fruits of his own diligence, and through a . . . liberal legislation the American citizen is protected against the tyranny of the authorities.

Hans Barlien,
A Norwegian immigrant,
writing in around 1837

The first main wave of Scandinavian immigrants in the early 19th century came for very American reasons. Like the British colonists who had come to New England two centuries earlier, they wanted freedom, especially religious freedom. Lutheranism, the national religion of the Scandinavian countries, was completely intertwined with the state. From a child's birth, all records were kept by the parish. Everyone was required to become confirmed in the church, being taught to read for the purpose. Laws were passed against their worshipping in any other faith.

Scandinavia had been a haven for religious refugees in earlier centuries. Protestant groups fled there from persecution in Europe just after the Reformation—that is, the massive swing from Catholicism to Protestantism that began in Northern Europe during the 16th century. But in the 18th and 19th centuries, the Lutheran Church had come to feel like something of a burden on the general population. The church required heavy taxes from parishioners, either in cash, kind, or labor, whether or not they wished to be active members of the church. The Lutheran clergy, being drawn from the privileged upper classes, failed to speak to the needs of the poorer majority. The time was ripe for simpler and popular revival movements, many of which would originate in other parts of the world.

One of the earliest of the successful popular movements was the American Temperance Movement, which was a model for many later social movements, notably in Sweden. Missionaries, many of them American, from the Methodist, Baptist, Mormon, Moravian, and other churches, had great success among the revival-hungry population.

Scandinavians also formed their own fundamentalist or revivalist movements, hoping to restore a supposedly purer form of religious worship to their countries. One national movement in Norway, for example, was led by popular revivalist Hans Nielsen Hauge. Haugeans believed that the members of the congregation—lay (untrained) Bible readers, rather than pastors with special training and authority—should control their own religious worship. Believing in the rights of individuals to make their own decision, Haugeans challenged the authority not only of the church but also of the state itself. Similar religious movements were found in other parts of Scandinavia.

Some Scandinavian movements went even further, desiring to establish communities in which all property and decision-making was shared. These utopian or communal movements were sharply frowned upon. Some emigrants later attempted to establish such ideal communities in America.

The Lutheran clergy sharply repressed this religious dissent in Scandinavia. With state encouragement, they began to enforce laws that had been on the books for many years, but had been neglected. Among them was a law forbidding private prayer meetings in the home, or anywhere other than in a Lutheran church under a state-approved pastor. Many of the earliest immigrants to America were religious dissidents who had been persecuted by the state-supported clergy.

So many people left for these reasons in the first half of the 19th century that the various Scandinavian governments bowed to pressure and liberalized the country's religious laws by mid-century. But America's freedom of religion, buttressed by the Bill of Rights' declaration of the separation of church and state, continued throughout the 19th century to appeal to Scandinavians of nonapproved religious movements.

These early, religiously motivated immigrants were trailblazers for other Scandinavians. For—as Hans Barlien noted in the quotation that headed this chapter—Scandinavian immigrants sought other freedoms as well.

Liberty, Equality, and Fraternity

In the 19th century, Sweden was the most powerful of the Scandinavian countries. In that century of strong nationalistic feelings both the Finns and the Norwegians wanted independence from the Swedes. Icelanders, too, desired freedom, for they were totally dependent on the rule of Denmark.

Intertwined with the question of self-rule was that of class. The Scandinavian countries had long been ruled by a rather small elite of nobles and powerful families, many of them tracing their positions back to previous centuries of empire. The poor farmers, fishers, and workers of all sorts had little say in the governing of their own countries. Property qualifications generally barred poorer people from voting or holding office.

Throughout Scandinavia, the established Lutheran religious leaders—who sometimes had elaborately decorated churches like this Norwegian one—lost touch with many poor parishioners and freethinkers.
(Library of Congress)

The ideas of Europe's 18th-century Enlightenment—ideas such as liberty, equality, and fraternity (brotherhood)—had inspired first the American and later the French revolutions. These ideas, and the model of freedom that existed in the United States, strongly stirred the general population of Scandinavia. The right of everyone to vote, the right to serve in the parliament, the right to be tried by a jury of peers, the right to bear arms, these and other such rights were powerful attractions to people who had few or none of them.

On a very personal level, in America no one had to "bow and scrape" before nobles or state officials; no one had to "doff his cap" to his supposed superiors. In America everyone was equal.

Immigrants would find the reality of America was not everything they had hoped. African slaves, after all, were not considered equal by the United States government. Nor were women, who were denied the right to vote.

But the ideas of liberty and equality still had enormous power. The strength of these ideas partly explains why so many Scandinavians flocked from abroad and from their new American homes to fight with Lincoln's Union army in the Civil War.

America Letters

Scandinavians learned about America in a variety of ways, but the most important of these were "America letters." The early Scandinavian settlers of colonial times set a pattern of writing letters to family and friends, describing the fertile land and the freedom to be found there. The relatively few Scandinavian immigrants to settle in the United States in the 18th and early 19th centuries continued the pattern of writing such America letters. So did later waves of immigrants, through the 19th and early 20th centuries.

Many America letters emphasized economic opportunity, stating (as did one Finnish writer) that even the poorest girl in America "walked the streets in silk, and with a hat on her head to boot." America's riches were often confirmed when immigrants enclosed with their letters money or prepaid tickets to America, and the message: "Come, join me!" By the late 19th century, photographs showing prosperous immigrants in their "Sunday best" gave additional confirmation of America's promise.

Some America letters exaggerated far beyond reality, of course. An

— 65 —

1,500,000 ACRES

ere udlagt Agerbrugsland, beliggende i Staten Nebraska i den saakaldte Platt: Riverdalen og bestaaende af udsøgt Sletteland med overflødigt Land, godt Klima og i Nærheden af Stæder og Jernbanestationer, med bekvem Adgang til Marked.

Større Fordele ere aldrig i noget Land i Verden tilbudne Emigranten og Nybyggeren.

Ved Siden af ovennævnte Jernbaneland findes endvidere i Nebraska

4.000.000 Acr. Guvernementsland

hvilket uddeles frit ifølge den saakaldte „Homestead" Lov — alt, hvad der er at betale for dette Land er $25.00 for Opmaaling, etc.

Dette er et Tilbud, som ei maa lades upaaagtet af Enhver, der eier en om kun liden og ubetydelig Kapital og vil forskaffe sig et eget Hjem i Nærheden af den store National-Jernbane, der er forsynet med alle de Bekvemmeligheder, som et gammelt bebygget Land tilbyder.

Beskrivelser, Cirkulærer og Karter sendes paa Anmodning til hvilkensomhelst Plads i de Forenede Stater, Canada og Europa. Breve med Forespørgsler blive sikkeltligt besvarede.

Adresse :

O. F. DAVIS,
LAND COMMISSIONER,
U. P. R. R. Co. Omaha, Nebraska.

Posters like this one, distributed from Omaha, Nebraska, by the Union Pacific Railroad, attracted many Scandinavians to settle on America's Great Plains.
(Author's archives)

1866 letter to Finland, for example, asserted that "in America even the grain grows up in a week." Also, they seldom described the real difficulties of starting life in a new land. But they exercised a powerful effect on their European readers.

"America fever" began building as a result of these letters, but relatively few Scandinavians immigrated to the United States before the mid-19th century. That was because Scandinavian governments would not allow citizens to leave the country without special approval, which they were reluctant to give.

But even before Scandinavians were free to travel, they followed with great interest the American Colonies' move toward independence. They not only received personal letters and read published reports, but they also sent some soldiers to fight in the Revolutionary War. Sweden, for example, sent 80 officers to fight for American independence (mostly enrolled in the forces of their French allies) and was one of the first countries to formally recognize the new United States.

Scandinavian republican sentiments were somewhat dampened by the violence that followed the French Revolution of 1789. The governments of Scandinavia, concerned by the possibility of revolution in their own lands, became sharply repressive. But the attraction of America remained undimmed.

Few Scandinavians traveled to America during the Napoleonic Wars of the late 18th and early 19th centuries. But peace in 1815 brought many more visitors to America and a further spread of literature about the country. Scandinavians were especially interested in Alexis De Tocqueville's *Democracy in America*, published in Sweden in 1839, only four years after its appearance in France. And many American novels circulated in Scandinavia in the 1830s, especially those of James Fenimore Cooper, which remained very popular into the 20th century.

So, all through these years, America fever grew. But no substantial numbers of emigrants could leave Scandinavia until about 1840. Travel restrictions were tightest in Sweden, Finland, and Iceland. Norwegians and Danes were somewhat freer. Cost also limited emigration. Even after travel restrictions were eased, the expense limited the number of emigrants until the 1850s and 1860s, when fares began to come down.

Visions of Freedom

The year 1848 was a year of revolutions in Europe. None was so violent or bloody—or successful—as the French and American revolutions. Still, these revolutions curbed the power of monarchs across Europe, and brought to many people the hope of a better, more equal society.

Inspired by visions of a new order, many Scandinavian groups left for America, hoping to establish a society completely of their own making. Many of them did not want to merge with the population of the United States, but to establish a "New Norway" or a " New Sweden" under the protection of the United States Bill of Rights. Internationally famous Norwegian violinist Ole Bull, for example, was inspired by the 1848 revolutions and a tour of America to found a short-lived "new Norway, dedicated to freedom, baptized in independence, and protected by the mighty flag of the Union." He was not alone, and numerous leaders carried such visions to the New World.

The revolutions of 1848 also had economic effects. With the countries of Europe in turmoil, the demand for goods like timber and iron—important Scandinavian exports—was low. Scandinavia, along with most of Europe, experienced widespread depression. Sailors, dockworkers, factory workers, builders, loggers, woodworkers, and the like were unemployed. Many of these looked to America for paying work, pure and simple.

California Gold

There was also the lure of gold. With the 1848 discovery of the precious metal at Sutter's Mill, near Sacramento, adventurers streamed to California, hoping to make their fortunes. Sailors on vessels of all flags jumped ship in San Francisco and other West Coast ports.

Many Scandinavians who went to California during the Gold Rush stopped only briefly and then returned home. Others came and stayed. Nor did all who had gone to California, even in the first year or two of the gold rush, strike it rich. Far from it.

But some did return home with a modest pile of gold, fanning the gold fever. A Norwegian man named Christian Poulsen, for example, happened to be in San Francisco in January 1848, as a ship's carpenter, when news came of the gold strike. By April 1849, he had arrived back home with a small fortune of over $9,000. He founded a shipbuilding and shipping firm in Norway, and all his life was known as the "gold man." Two Swedish sailors, Johan Björkgreen and Johan Petersen, returned home from California similarly laden with gold; they reported seeing many fellow Scandinavians at the California diggings.

In addition to these firsthand reports, letters, books, and pamphlets were soon flooding Scandinavia and all Europe, telling the best routes for reaching California. Many who might otherwise never have left home were lured to America by tales of gold strikes.

Recruiting Agents

In the mid-19th century, recruiters also spread throughout Scandinavia, seeking to sign up potential emigrants. Some of these recruiters worked for shipping lines, which had begun to see the profit to be made from passengers' fares. Norwegians seem to have led the way in emigrant recruiting. In 1843, several ship's captains operating out of Bergen were accused of "soul buying" by the local newspapers.

Local authorities were often quite unhappy about recruiting efforts, and newspapers warned the unwary. A Finnish paper said of recruiters: "Their promises are pure lies and a fraud. The recruiters are seeking simple-minded folk to fall into their trap. Men of Finland, keep your eyes open." The warning was certainly justified in regard to shipping recruiters, who notoriously exaggerated the supposed virtues of their ships.

Employment recruiters, too, would sometimes lie and exaggerate to get Scandinavians to come to America to fill jobs. Such recruiters were employed by American business firms, such as railroad lines or mining companies, which desperately needed workers. But since many of the would-be emigrants were unemployed, they often benefitted greatly by going to America—exaggerations or not.

Many recruiters found the way already prepared for them by the America letters. Oscar Malmborg, a Swedish soldier who had served in the United States Army during the Mexican War, worked as an agent for the Illinois Central Railroad, recruiting people to settle along the railroad's right of way. (The railroad hoped that the settlers would ship farm products on the company's tracks, thus generating business for the line). When Malmborg arrived in Wrigstad, Sweden, in February 1861, he found that the people there had already heard he was coming. They packed the 2,000-seat church so tightly that, "I could scarcely move my arms but a still greater number had to remain in the yard." Many local farmers, on hearing Malmborg was coming, had already sold their farms and were packing to leave for America.

Still other agents were employed by state governments, which wanted settlers to open up their wilderness lands. During the second half of the 19th century, many states such as Wisconsin, Minnesota, Michigan, and Maine had active recruitment programs attractive to Scandinavians. They often provided jobs, land, and help in making the journey.

In the 1860s, even the federal government of the United States was active in recruiting. Washington wanted not only settlers, but also soldiers—to fight in the Union army during the Civil War. What it had to offer was spelled out in the Homestead Act of 1862. This act, which would change the face of the American plains, promised free land in the West—160 acres of it—to those who would come, live on it, and work it. President Abraham Lincoln sent 30 American consular officials to Sweden alone to publicize the Homestead Act of 1862. Swedish immigrant Axel Jarlson, writing years later in *The Independent* (Vol LV, January 8, 1903), recalled the clear promise: "In America they gave you good land for nothing, and in two years you could be a rich man."

The response to Lincoln's recruiting effort was so great—especially after a series of crop failures in Sweden—that the Swedish government issued a general warning against emigration in wartime. Many of these immigrants were persuaded to join the Union Army or to act as support personnel during the Civil War, before settling on their homesteads. The Confederate States, with some justification, complained that they were fighting a European army solicited under orders of "Lincoln & Company."

These were the most powerful attractions in America. But there were also some major pressures building in Scandinavia. Most important was a rapidly rising population, caused partly by the lowering of the death rate after the introduction of the smallpox vaccine. In rural areas, already-small farms were divided even further among a larger number of children, until the tiny plots could no longer support so many.

Scandinavian farmers also had lost some of the market for their grain. As the American and Russian wheat fields began to produce large amounts of grain in the 19th century, the two nations could supply Europe more cheaply than could Scandinavians, with their marginal farms. Some farmers, especially in Denmark, responded by switching to dairy farming or by raising livestock. But most simply became poorer.

All over Scandinavia landless laborers, especially young men, went begging for work. They went to the cities, of course, but the cities could not absorb them either. Many looked to America for hope of a free and prosperous life.

Meanwhile, in each of the Scandinavian countries special conditions led to the migration of large numbers of the population.

The Swedes

Unlike most countries, Sweden had traditionally experienced more immigration than emigration. But in the 19th century, Sweden was undergoing enormous changes. A population of about 3,000,000 in 1815 would double by 1900, then rise by half again to over 8,000,000 in 1970—all despite the loss of over a million emigrants, 98% of them to North America.

Coupled with this rapid population increase was a substantial shift in population, partly caused by an enclosure movement. Under the old farming system, land was held in common by a village, and the pieces worked by each farmer were scattered around the area. In the 1820s, the Swedish government enclosed these areas, making small individual farms and depopulating many small villages.

With both enclosure and a rapidly rising population, many people found themselves landless laborers, able to work—if at all—only as tenants or hired hands. Many migrated to the cities to work in the new factories—or left Sweden altogether. As recently as 1870, 90 percent of the population lived on farms. This was down to 75 percent in 1900 and only 20 percent in the 1970s.

This combination of rapid population growth, enclosure movements, urbanization, and industrialization disrupted Swedish society. And it created large numbers of people who were cut loose from the land and wanted to seek their fortunes elsewhere.

The Finns

As a part of Sweden until the early 19th century, Finland experienced some of the same changes, though in a somewhat less drastic way. But Finland also experienced some quite different and devastating changes of its own.

When the Russians took over in 1809, the Finns had hopes for more independence. Unlike the Swedes, the Russians initially allowed the Finns relative freedom in ruling themselves. In 1812, they even returned to Finland the Karelian lands lost in the previous century's wars. But most of the riches and the power still belonged to the upper- and middle-class Swedish-speakers, not to the poorer Finnish-speakers.

Under these conditions, Finnish nationalism bloomed. Much of the focus was on the Finnish language. Though the majority of the population spoke Finnish, Swedish had long been the only official language of government and education. Among cultured, educated people, few except the clergy spoke Finnish—and that to communicate with their parishioners. Given this low status and lack of Finnish readers, few books were published in the language.

Then, in the early 19th century, Finns began to call for higher status for the Finnish language. Adolf Ivan Arwidsson, professor at the University of Turku, was an early leader in the movement. In 1835, Elias Lönnrot published a book of Finnish folklore, *Kalevala*, drawing on the old Finnish oral traditions—which the Swedish-speaking elite had not thought worth preserving. This helped Finns develop a new pride in their culture. But the fight to gain respect for Finnish language and culture was a long one. Not until 1902 was the Finnish language finally proclaimed as officially equal with Swedish in national life and routinely used in government, schools, and cultural organizations.

In some parts of the country, Finnish nationalism expressed itself in a reaction against the Swedish-dominated, state Lutheran Church. Revivalists such as Lars Levi Laestadius called for a purified, more fundamentalist church, and won a good deal of support in rural areas. By the 1860s some of Laestadius's followers had immigrated to northern Norway, where they fished, farmed, and mined copper. Some other Finns immigrated to Alaska, then held by Russia.

As elsewhere in Scandinavia, life was changing on the land. While in 1815 half of Finland's farmers owned their own land, by the turn of the century that figure was down to less than one quarter. Most Finns were farmers, often tenant farmers or laborers. But the population more than tripled in the 19th century, to nearly three million, far more than the land could support. Later, as the government moved to put small farms together into larger holdings, many of these people were forced off the land altogether.

Many unemployed, landless laborers moved toward construction and factory work in cities—far too many. Southern Finns worried about these "beggers who go from house to house to seek their livelihood." So it was that many left the country altogether for far-off places like Australia and Brazil, many for Canada, and most for the United States.

In some parts of Finland, people forced off farmland could move readily into the lumbering industry, which was booming in the late 19th century. But in some regions along the Gulf of Bothnia, no workable forests remained; loggers and tarworkers, who had once worked there, headed westward. The Finnish ports of Bothnia might once have been shipbuilding centers, but by the late 19th century, old wooden sailing ships were gradually being replaced by larger metal-hulled steamships built elsewhere. So shipbuilders, too, joined the parade to America. It is no accident that the majority of Finnish immigrants to the United States came from Bothnia.

During this period, Finland was also shifting into the modern world. New factories, especially for making textiles and wood products, were being built in the cities. But the benefits were still unequally distributed between Swedes and Finns. So, like workers in industries elsewhere, Finns actively organized labor movements. Many Finnish labor leaders were inspired by America, visited there, and urged their workers to build a new and better life in America. One such leader, Matti Kurikka, wrote in *Työmies (The Worker)*:

We shall discover the historical salvation of our people through emigration. In Finland the working class may eat only raw herring and drink skimmed milk. Everything is much better in America.

Finns began to emigrate in large numbers later than most other Scandinavians, partly because they were farther away and did not have such ready access to word of America. But once they learned of the opportunities offered by the new land, Finnish workers became far less tolerant of conditions in their own land and left in droves.

Finland's heavy emigration started in the 1860s, partly because of some changes in Russia's policy toward Finland. In the late 19th century, Russia was in the grip of its own nationalist movement, and tried to merge Finland into the empire. It proposed Russian as the official language and attempted to suppress the Finnish free press. It also tried to replace the Lutheran Church with the Russian Eastern Orthodox form of Christianity. It even began to draft Finns into the Russian army, which had not been done before. This caused many young Finnish men to emigrate.

The government tried to stem the flow of emigrants by refusing them passports, but many simply left with false papers. Among those who stayed, some prepared for armed rebellion. Since Finland had no army, some young Finns joined the German army to gain military training for a Finnish revolution.

As Russia moved toward revolution and civil war, so did Finland. Finnish fighters were divided between the White Guards, mostly nonsocialists who had urged passive resistance against the Russians, and the Red Guards, mostly socialists who wanted not just independence but also a more sweeping social revolution along Russian lines. In May 1918, the White Guards, supported by Germany and including many German-trained young Finns, finally won over the Russian-supported Red Guards. In 1919 a republic was proclaimed, under a reconciliation president.

Even so, Finnish emigration continued until the 1920s, when the United States set a restrictive quota, and the 1930s, when the Great Depression set in.

The Norwegians

In Norway, the population began to grow in the 18th century. Many new farms were cleared, providing additional living space and jobs for the larger population. But there still was not enough work available. Many unemployed young people wandered around the country, forming bands of migrant laborers for seasonal work, especially harvest times. There were so many migrants that the government would sometimes have "vagrant hunts," in which they rounded up these wandering workers and put them into prisons or workhouses.

Some of these unemployed workers migrated to the seacoast in looking for work. They frequently found it in seasonal fishing expeditions, often on ships based in the Netherlands. Many of these workers eventually settled in Dutch cities, such as Amsterdam, joining local Lutheran congregations and often marrying Dutch women. Norwegian women also migrated to the Netherlands, generally to work as servants. So Norwegians, by the time of the American Revolution, had set something of a pattern in migration that would later be turned toward America.

The people of Norway as yet knew little of America. But as the country grew more prosperous in the late 18th century and increased its ties with other European countries, Norwegians began to learn about this new land. Because they were unhappy under the Danish monarchy, many Norwegians were especially interested in the American Colonies' fight for independence from European control. Norway's shipping began to revive in this period, and its sailors once more began traveling the Atlantic in large numbers.

As France's ally in the Napoleonic Wars, the Norwegians took several American ships, even though the United States was neutral. The prizes and their crews were laid up in Norwegian harbors, such as Christiansand. Through contacts like these, people along the Norwegian coast began to learn more about America and Americans.

Also during the Napoleonic Wars, many Norwegian ships were captured and held in British ports. Visited in prison by English Quakers, some of the sailors converted to the new religion, and took it home with them after the war. In at least two ports—Christiania (now Oslo) and Stavanger—there were enough of them to establish a Society of Friends, as the Quaker congregations are called. Through the international network of Quakers, these Norwegian converts learned of the religious freedom enjoyed in the United States. Because the Norwegian state Lutheran Church disapproved of these Quakers, they were among the first to immigrate to America. Not for some decades, until 1845, did the Norwegian government grant religious freedom to Quakers and others who wished to worship outside the Lutheran Church.

In 1817, 500 German emigrants bound for the United States were marooned in Bergen when their ship was damaged. While they badgered the Norwegian government into helping them continue their journey to America, they got in touch with some of Norway's religious dissidents. Through such contacts, word of America spread rather widely.

By the spring of 1818, rumors were circulating in eastern Norway that a ship lay ready in Christiania to take immigrants to America, offering free transportation and food, free land, a house, and cattle in the new land, and free return passage for anyone who was dissatisfied. By late summer, with a peasant revolt stirring in the land, the government was offering a reward for the identity of those who spread such rumors. Some people—it is not clear how many—believed the rumors and made their way to Christiania, hoping to board ship. Despite their disappointment, word of America kept growing.

Between the late 1600s and 1815, Norway's population had more than doubled, to 886,000. It continued to grow at a high rate, causing ever greater pressure for emigration. The government tried to break up farms into smaller plots, but many tenant farmers found they simply could not make a living off the land. The problem was compounded by high land taxes and, in the 1830s especially, by crop failures and widespread famine.

Times were especially hard in Norway after the Napoleonic Wars, when shipping suffered greatly. Until 1849, Britain's Navigation Act required that trade goods, including Scandinavian timber, be carried in British ships, wherever possible. This threw many Norwegian sailors out of work.

There was also pressure for more freedom within Norway, especially among the small farmers. In 1814, after shifting from Danish to Swedish rule, Norway established a new "free constitution," in response to political pressure from the population, which had had few rights before then. In 1830, Norway became the first of the Scandinavian countries to do away with titles of nobility. Farmers gained a voice in the Norwegian parliament, the Storting, and political leaders like Ole Gabriel Ueland called for a "true government of the people." Others, such as Henrik Wergeland, focused on social and economic issues, calling for land reform, reform of prisons, better sanitation, temperance, and adequate housing for workers. Wergeland knew of and admired America, but he hoped to improve his land so that its inhabitants would not feel they had to emigrate to make a better life. In the 1850s, Johan Sverdrup campaigned for a jury system on the American or British model.

And conditions *did* improve. As Britain gradually removed restrictions on shipping, Norwegian shipping revived. Norway as a whole became freer and more prosperous. But it was not enough.

In the years after Europe's revolutions of 1848, many Norwegians worked hard and long for reform in their homeland. Marcus Thrane was perhaps the best known of these reformers, a free thinker and a socialist who hoped to establish full social equality and evenhanded justice in Norway. But both the state and the church objected to his activities and imprisoned him and a number of his followers. On their release from prison, some of them, including Thrane himself, immigrated to America. They were followed by many other Thranites, especially landless farm laborers from eastern Norway and Trøndelag. In the years that followed, as transatlantic fares dropped, they were followed by many other Norwegians, especially the poor, the landless, and the jobless.

World-famous Norwegian violinist Ole Bull sponsored an idealistic settlement in America in the early 19th century.
(Library of Congress)

The Danes

Large-scale migration started rather late among Danes. In the decades when Northern Europeans were first settling the east coast of North America, Denmark was still a major power in the world. True, it had by then lost much of the Scandinavian territory it had once held. But Norway, Iceland, Greenland, and the region of Skåne (in what is now Sweden) all were under Danish rule in this period.

Denmark itself was more prosperous than other Scandinavian countries. People there had more work, better pay, and somewhat more freedom. The Danish government was rather liberal, and it strongly supported the small farmers. In the 19th century, when many other parts of Scandinavia were undergoing enclosure movements, making large farms from small pieces, Denmark was doing the reverse, breaking up large farms to create more small holdings for the rising population. The government also encouraged dairy farming and the raising of animals, both of which were more profitable than grain and vegetable farming. It also encouraged cooperative movements among the farmers.

As a result, the early relatively few Danish immigrants to America were generally skilled, educated people, often from the cities seeking opportunity in a wider world. Few were poor farmers hoping for a new and better life—the image that fits much of the rest of Scandinavian emigration.

Some, especially in the 18th and early 19th centuries, were religious dissidents, looking for freedom to worship in their own way, rather than in the prescribed Lutheran form. Though the Lutheran Church in Denmark was not as strict and repressive as in other Scandinavian countries, many Danes were still open to new religions. When colonies were established by these new religious groups, some Danes emigrated to join them.

But gradually Denmark's power declined. In 1814, Denmark shared in the defeat of its ally, Napoleonic France, losing Norway to Sweden. Even so, for a time the Danish government managed rather well. Through the first half of the 19th century, a liberal government introduced many reforms. The new constitution of 1849 gave far more people the right to vote and allowed freedom of worship. A "folk-school" movement, started by Bishop N.F. S. Grundtvig in the early part of the century, brought more education to rural children.

But in the 1860s, all that changed. After an unsuccessful war with

Prussia and Austria in 1864, Denmark lost one-quarter of its land, notably the prime farming region of Schleswig, in the southern part of the Jutland Peninsula. Danes from these lost territories fled to the United States in large numbers, rather than be drafted into the German army. In Denmark itself, a conservative government took over in 1866, scrapping many of the reforms in the national constitution. Meanwhile, the population continued to rise, leading to widespread unemployment in both country and city.

So it was that many Danes were attracted to America from the late 1860s on. They heard of the new land from other Scandinavians who had gone before. The possibility of "limitless land," the ability for even poor people to vote and hold office, and the promises of work and plentiful food—all these were powerful attractions. And they formed quite a contrast with conditions in Denmark. One immigrant in the early 19th century wrote that American farmers were generous with both food and pay for their harvest workers, not like "those long-fingered, proud noblemen in Denmark, who feed their harvest people on salt herring and barley pudding seven hundred and twenty times a year." Recruiting agents, who worked all through Scandinavia, became especially active in Denmark in this period.

The Icelanders

Icelanders came to the United States for many of the same reasons as other Scandinavians. First among these was religion. Many Icelanders had become disenchanted with the state church, Lutheranism. (It had been forced on them, despite an armed protest, by the Danish king in 1550.) They particularly resented the heavy taxes they were forced to pay to support the church. By the mid-19th century some Icelanders had converted to other religions. A few who had adopted Mormonism were drawn to join the large Mormon settlements in Utah. Some other religious dissenters followed.

Many other Icelanders were unhappy with their island's colonial status. For centuries, Denmark had held Iceland in a tight grip. From 1602, no other countries were allowed to trade with Iceland. And Icelanders had no shipping of their own, no independent line of contact with the outside world. Isolated, Iceland grew steadily poorer, and its population dropped markedly, to a low point of 45,000 in the early 1800s.

Even though the island was isolated, some Icelanders were educated in Denmark and brought home new theories from Europe. So the ideas of nationalism that abounded in Europe in the 19th century began to spread in Iceland, too. The result was a call for independence. Denmark responded in 1874 by allowing Iceland somewhat more self-rule than it had had before. But that was too little, too late, for many 19th-century Icelanders.

As word of America's prosperity filtered back to Iceland, many Icelanders emigrated for the hope of freedom and a better economic life. The pull was so strong that, between 1870 and 1900, and in spite of occasional depression in the United States, about 20 percent of Iceland's total population of about 75,000 immigrated to North America, some to Canada and some to the United States.

After 1900, however, few Icelanders emigrated. And for good reason. In 1918, Iceland became a separate state, no longer a colony, though still tied to the Danish crown. Then in 1944, Iceland broke with Denmark altogether and became a fully independent republic. With these increases in self-rule, Iceland began to flourish. In the first three quarters of the 20th century, Iceland's population tripled to well over 210,000. In the same period, many Icelanders moved from the countryside to the cities, especially to the capital of Reykjavik.

Icelanders today have one of the highest literacy rates and highest standards of living in the world. Problems of slums, crime, and extreme poverty are practically unknown there. After World War II, some Icelandic war brides came to the United States with husbands who had been stationed on the island as soldiers. But most Icelanders in the 20th century have elected to stay in their homeland.

Chains of Immigrants

Like immigrants the world over, Scandinavians generally came to America through chains of referrals. A sailor or adventurer who had seen the wonderous lands abroad sent word back to those at home: the famous "America letters." Soon these "pathfinders" would be followed by brothers, cousins, fathers, sisters, whole families, parts of villages and provinces. Sometimes so many people came at once or over a few years from one place, that the immigrants to some extent recreated their old communities in the new world.

Swedish immigrant Axel Jarlson, writing in *The Independent* (Vol. LV, January 8, 1903), described the typical immigrant chain:

> My uncle Olaf [who had been to America often on the ships] used to come to us between voyages, and he was all the time talking about America; what a fine place it was to make money in. . . . A man who had been living in America once came to visit the little village that was near our cottage. He wore gold rings set with jewels and had a fine watch. He said that food was cheap in America and that a man could earn nearly ten times as much there as in Sweden. . . . There seemed to be no end to his money. . . . It was after this that father and mother were both sick during all of one winter, and we had nothing to eat. . . . We had to sell our cows. . . . So at last it was decided that my brother was to go to America.

So the chain would begin. Axel's brother Gustaf was the first to go to Minnesota, on a ticket paid for by their uncle Olaf. Two years later sailed another brother, Eric, followed by two sisters, Hilda and Christine, and finally Axel and his sister Helene. The men each got 60-acre farms from the government, and the women got "work in families of Minneapolis, and soon were earning almost as much as my brothers." By the time Axel arrived, his elder sister Hilda was married and living in a large brick house, with two servants and a carriage.

So whole families made their way to America. Most did not prosper as quickly as the Jarlsons. But enough did to keep alive the dream for hundreds of thousands of would-be immigrants.

4

Voyage to the New World

*It seems so strange to me when I think that more than seven years
have passed since I have seen you all; it seems it could not have been
a quarter of that time. I can see so clearly the last glimpse I had of
Mamma, standing alone amid all the tracks at Eslöv station. Oliva I
last saw sitting on her sofa in her red and black dress, holding little
Brita, one month old, on her lap. And Wilhelm I last saw in Lund at
the station, as he rolled away with the train, waving his last farewell
to me. . . .*

*Ida Lindgren, Swedish immigrant,
writing from Manhattan, Kansas, 1877*

From the farms and the small villages, from the craggy mountains and
deep fjords, from the suburbs and the streets of the towns, emigrants
headed for the main ports to America. Because of travel restrictions,
people who wished to emigrate generally needed a travel permit from the
local authorities and a certificate from the pastor of the local parish for a
passport. Only after the mid-19th century, when restrictions were eased,
could emigration begin in earnest.

Many emigrants chose to start their journey in spring or early summer.
Axel Jarlson, for example, left in April because his uncle had told him that
"this was the time to start, because work on the farms there [in America]
was just beginning." In the late 19th and early 20th centuries, port cities
even had something of a season for migrations. Norwegian poet Aasmund
Vinje, writing in the 1850s, noted:

Now it is again that time of year when the emigrants are to be seen in the streets, and ships are being rigged, and water casks are being made for the trip to America. . . . This is just as regular as the coming of the cuckoo, and the one is as much a part of the order of nature as the other.

Travelers were warned against arriving during the cold weather. Writing from America in March 1890, Finnish immigrant Nikolai Nieminen told a friend, "there are now again good times here in the summertime, but no one should come during the winter or his skin would soon wither and cling to his backbone." Immigrants heading for lumbering country in America, however, would often travel during September, for logging teams began work in the autumn.

Leaving Home

Many emigrants were given special farewell parties by friends and family before they left. One Finnish emigrant described the leavetaking in the Finnish-American newspaper *Työmies* (*The Worker*), July 29, 1891:

Because of it we walked around in our Sunday clothes for a week, and didn't do the daily chores. "What need have we to work when we will soon be going to America," so we thought and walked around with cigarettes in our teeth saying goodbye to friends, who wished us a good trip and shook our hands warmly. And finally the awaited day came when we had to say goodbye to the home folks, but that was hardest of all . . . From the churchyard hill we turned around and looked at the village and a strange feeling arose in the breast, which finally burst into a sigh, but we continued our journey . . .

Before the second half of the 19th century, when liners began providing food and bedding, emigrants had to pack enough provisions to last them for a two- to three-month voyage. Generally they chose herring and salted or dried meat, such as pork or mutton, butter, whey cheese, grain, potatoes, flour, flatbread (unleavened bread), and sometimes even brandy or beer. In addition, they had to take cooking utensils, pots and pans, blankets, and sheepskin coverlets. Some early emigrants also took with them some tools for use in the new land. Norwegian Jon Ellingbø brought with him all the equipment he needed to set up as a blacksmith. His countryman Knut Norsving brought not only a wagon, but also two

This 19th-century liner advertises that it will take passengers from several ports in Norway and Denmark, then travel to America via Glasgow, Scotland. (Author's archives)

enormous millstones. Everything else—house and land, furnishings, tools, and livestock—had to be sold before leaving.

Later emigrants generally traveled lighter. By then it was clear that they could find whatever tools they needed in America. And by then food and bedding were being provided on board ship, though emigrants still had to provide for themselves during the days or weeks before they reached the transatlantic liner—and after they landed in America. Young men and women usually carried little beyond food and clothing, in a trunk or a small bag slung over a shoulder. Finnish emigrant Nestori Kuuisto took only some bread, cured mutton, tobacco, and extra underwear when he left for America in 1902. But even emigrants who had things of value—crystals, fine silver, and such—often left them behind.

Generally the journey started with a cart ride to the nearest main town—in the mid-19th century, generally to the railroad station. Parting with family and friends was sad, but for many of the emigrants—especially the young ones, out to see the world on their own—it was also a joyous occasion. They would sometimes be found by the tens and even the hundreds on the trains, laughing and singing. The young Finnish man who told his story in *Työmies* describes how it was:

When we were all inside the train, the conductor's shrill whistle sounded and we left . . . we sang with all our strength, so that the conductor asked us to sing a little quieter, so we would not cause a disturbance on the train, then we settled down a bit, but again after we had left the station some one started a song and then the others joined in right away . . .

Early Crossings

In the early days of Scandinavian emigration, before the mid-19th century, no regularly scheduled liners existed to carry passengers to America. Most emigrants were forced to travel in groups and had to make special arrangements for passage. Sometimes they actually bought their own ship to take them across the ocean. Young, healthy men, of course, always had the option of signing on as sailors, and then leaving their ship in an American port. Many did, and it was the main form of Scandinavian migration from the mid-17th to the early 19th century. Not until the mid-19th century was transatlantic travel regular enough so that emigrants could travel alone or in small parties.

Emigrants in these early times paid for space in what were actually oceangoing cargo ships. Unfortunately, these ships had no schedule, but waited in port until they had enough cargo—including emigrants—to fill the ship. This meant that emigrants sometimes had to wait for weeks, in a land where they might not speak the language, before they could book passage. In 1846, for example, 300 Norwegians slept for several weeks out in the open, curled together "in tightly closed knots, in an atmosphere tainted by the stench rising from the marshy soil under the influence of the hot sun." Some would-be emigrants spent all their money in European ports and had to be sent home at the government's expense.

And when they did manage to book passage, space was almost all that they got—space, water, and wood for fires. No food; no beds. For such "accommodations" emigrants paid from $30 to $35 (in hard coin, not paper) in 1840 for the trip from Norway to America—in a period when a hired farm laborer in Norway might make $10 a year in cash.

Even when large-scale emigration began in the mid-19th century, many transatlantic travelers were still crossing the ocean in cargo ships that left from the smaller Scandinavian ports. In April 1853, 10 ships carrying Norwegian passengers left from Christiana Fjord alone. Because Norway had close shipping ties with Canada many of these ships took the Quebec

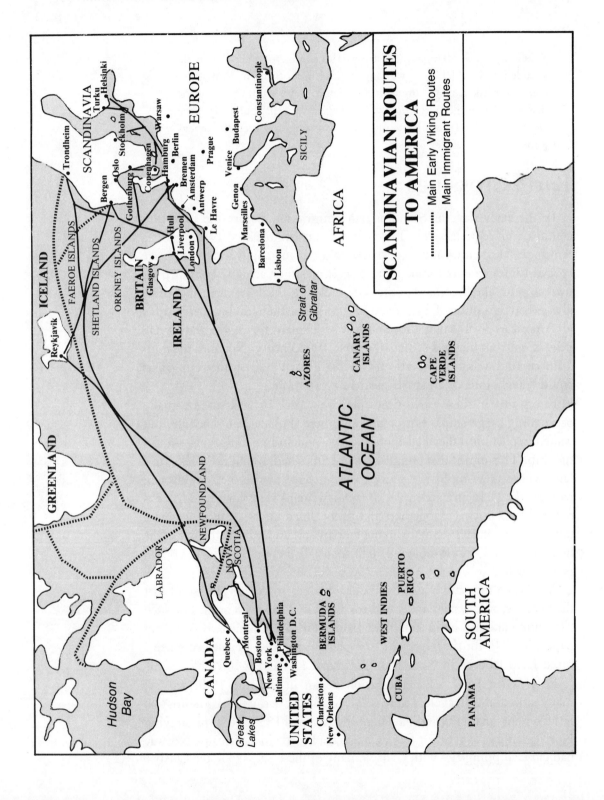

route. Soon fares were lowered to between $12 and $15 from Norway to Quebec.

Some ships began to advertise a special, large airy room between decks, built just for emigrants. The ships were still small and crude, but now they at least had rows of straw-filled bunks—meant for five people a bunk—in the large between-decks room where the emigrants ate, slept, and were sheltered from bad weather.

When health and weather permitted, emigrants would go up on deck for fresh air, exercise, and even dancing or wrestling. Otherwise, that room was their world for some eight to twelve weeks. In rough seas, the hatches would be closed and the air would get close and stale. Diseases of various kinds, if once brought abroad ship, could easily spread in such close quarters and with poor sanitation.

Few ships did not have at least one death at sea. Some emigrants seem to have accepted this as a matter of course. One Norwegian immigrant wrote in 1851: "Everything went well and happily for the passengers aboard, if we accept that we had seven deaths on the trip over." Because of the number of deaths at sea, both the United States and Canada passed ever-stronger laws requiring a minimum amount of space per immigrant on a ship. Scandinavian countries were slower to act; the Norwegian parliament rejected such a bill until 1863. When emigration was heavy, ship's captains simply jammed more people into the already tight quarters. In 1861 alone, 200 Norwegian emigrants died at sea.

Later Routes

But such small ships out of Scandinavian ports could not begin to handle the flood of emigrants that began in the 1850s and increased in the following decades. In 1853 and 1854, for example, the Swedish port of Gothenburg was thronged with many more emigrants than it could handle. As a result many emigrants had to make their way to one of the major Atlantic ports, such as Liverpool, England; Le Havre, France; or later Hamburg or Bremerhaven, Germany. Only there could they pick up an oceangoing vessel for the crossing to America.

For many emigrants, getting to the Atlantic ports involved several steps. Until the late 19th century, for example, Finns left from one of the Finnish ports and crossed the Baltic Sea, generally to Stockholm, Sweden. Then, joined by Swedish emigrants, they would cross the country by train to Gothenburg, the major port of emigration for Finns and Swedes in the mid-19th century. From there, they would head across the North Sea to Hull, on the east coast of England, and then go by train to the main port of Liverpool.

Danes in these years generally gathered at Copenhagen. Norwegians left from several ports, such as Bergen, Stavanger, or Christiana (Oslo). Both Danes and Norwegians often headed for Liverpool, but many went to Le Havre. Icelanders had to make a long detour from their homeland eastward, generally to Liverpool, before sailing back west across the ocean to America.

In the late 19th century, when German shipping lines became active in the transatlantic service, many Scandinavians picked up their transatlantic liners at Hamburg or Bremerhaven. Swedish or Finnish emigrants, for example, might go from Stockholm by ship to Lübeck, Germany, then head either overland by train or by ship via Copenhagen, to Hamburg or Bremerhaven.

The Finland Steamship Company began to sail directly between Hanko, Finland, and Hull, England, starting in late 1891. From then until World War I, this was the main route for Finnish emigrants.

To the Atlantic Ports

Whatever their home port, emigrants would board a small "coaster" that would take them toward the great Atlantic ports. These coasters were actually cargo ships, carrying products like codliver oil, timber, iron, or salt herring. They were not built for any real passenger trade. The departure from the homeland was always bittersweet, even though the air was often "filled with hurrahs" as the boat pulled away from shore. Few emigrants would see their homes and families again. And conditions on these crowded coasters were far from comfortable. A Finnish immigrant described how it was, leaving home to cross the Baltic, in *Työmies* (June 24, 1891):

> The evening began to grow dusk, everyone watched, did the coast of our dear Finland still wax blue on the horizon; night fell and with the night came a storm, everyone had to go down into the hold. Each sought out a sleeping berth, but in vain. They had to sleep on the floor, since there was no other place. . . . Many were not able to get up, what filth there was there, in Finland not even pigs lived in that

kind of smell, and what was still worse it was so tight we had to lay on top of each other, since we were somewhere around 200 and it was one small "hold" where we were.

Those heading for Liverpool had to cross the North Sea. For many emigrants this leg of the journey was the worst. A Finnish immigrant described the situation in *Sankarin Maine* (April 18, 1879):

Each shipping line [had] its own section, the boundaries of which were, however, no more than thick chalk marks, and thus travellers would wade in each other's vomit, which is abundant on the North Sea; and for this reason this is the worst section of the trip to America.

Accommodations were somewhat more comfortable in later years, especially just before World War I. But even so, during storms there was little to do—in the words of one immigrant—but play cards, sing hymns, and pray.

Emigrants from around the Baltic Sea made their way to Swedish ports like this one, and then on to the Atlantic ports.
(Library of Congress)

Booking Passage

When large-scale travel began in mid-19th century, travelers generally bought tickets for the stages of their journey piecemeal, purchasing their transatlantic tickets at ports such as Gothenburg or Stockholm. In the newspaper, *Sankarin Maine* (October 8, 1880), a Finnish immigrant describes the scene on arrival at Stockholm:

> . . . a great tumult arose, when the gangplanks of the ship were lowered; so many people rushed from the dock onto the ship that there was no room to move. They asked and pumped us about tickets . . . and we heard one and another selling their favors in both Swedish and Finnish.

Later in the century, when recruiters were seeking emigrants, and shipping companies vied for passengers even more actively, tickets covering the whole journey were sold at ticket offices in many parts of Scandinavia, sometimes even on the trains. Agents often met incoming trains and fought to bring unticketed passengers to their company's ticket offices.

Of course, many emigrants—a third or more in some Scandinavian countries—were sent a prepaid ticket by someone already in America. In Sweden in the mid-1880s, over half of the emigrants left on prepaid tickets. In the early 1870s, 40 percent of all Norwegians used prepaid tickets. In Denmark between 1877 and 1895, the proportion using prepaid tickets was about one-third, as it was in Finland. The poorer the emigrants' social group, the more likely they were to depend on receiving a prepaid ticket. In the years following heavy migration, the number of prepaid tickets increased sharply, as people sent tickets back home for their relatives—especially wives and children following husbands—or friends. But during years of depression in America, fewer tickets were sent back.

Many young men sent back to Scandinavia for a wife, sometimes someone they had known at home, but often someone who was selected for them. Many young single women accepted prepaid tickets to America, agreeing to marry the sender when they arrived at their destination. Some have described this as "matchmaking emigration."

The cost of tickets varied widely over the years. Ticket prices fell sharply in the 1880s, when many steamship lines were competing for passengers. Even though prices rose again afterwards, steamship companies had periodic "price wars," in 1889 and 1904, for example. Then, on the eve of World War I, prices soared again.

At the Atlantic Ports

At stations and ports along the way travelers found hotels catering especially to emigrants. Conditions were variable, but generally poor. Emigrants were, after all, a onetime, almost captive clientele.

For emigrants from rural areas, ports—especially large ones like Liverpool or Le Havre—were bustling, crowded places, quite confusing and even disturbing after the slow pace of country life. Many rightly worried about how to safeguard their small amount of funds, generally deciding to carry it in belts under their shirts or in pouches around their necks—even though robbers, knowing emigrants' habits, would look there first.

Port cities held other dangers for travelers, too. As people flooded through them, from all parts of Europe, disease sometimes ran wild. In 1853, more than 20 Danish Mormon children died of cholera in Liverpool, as their party passed through on the way to Utah.

By contrast, the emigrant facilities in Hamburg and Bremerhaven were models of their kind. From 1891 on, shipping lines were required by U.S. law to examine, vaccinate, and disinfect all immigrants carried on their ships. Any immigrant rejected by United States immigration inspectors would be returned at the shipping line's expense. Even so, many lines did only a slapdash job. But the German lines set up emigrant villages at Hamburg and Bremerhaven, where emigrants were housed in clean quarters, with food and bathing facilities—even hospitals—provided.

Packets and Liners

Liverpool was the preferred port in the mid-19th century because it had a longstanding transatlantic packet service, put in place to handle earlier emigrants and general traffic between the British Isles and America. Packets were boats sailing at regular schedules, regardless of whether the cabins or holds were all occupied—unlike earlier ships that waited in port until they had a full load of cargo. Packets were also specifically designed to carry passengers and light cargo, such as mail, not heavy goods, such as lumber or iron.

The first transatlantic packet out of Liverpool had gone into service in 1815. By 1829, there were three packets a week sailing between New York and Liverpool and Le Havre; two a month sailed between New York and London; and one a month between Boston and Liverpool. Packets sailed regularly, but less often, between New York and Hamburg, and between Baltimore and Liverpool.

Even so, these packets had little in the way of accommodation. People with money occupied the cabins. Poorer passengers—most emigrants—were simply placed in "steerage," a large below-decks area so named because it was near the ship's steering mechanism. Even in the 1860s many emigrants still traveled in cargo ships, but packets were the wave of the future, and they gradually took over the transatlantic service.

After 1865, conditions improved. Major steamship lines began to offer many more regularly scheduled sailings. Emigrants, knowing the time of departure, did not need to wait for days or weeks arranging for tickets. These liners also offered much quicker passage, better accommodations, and free food on board.

Even so, accommodations for the poorest passengers were awful. Most of these third class passengers still traveled steerage. A Finnish immigrant writing in *Sankarin Maine* (April 18, 1879), described the dismayed reaction of the travelers:

> The agent took all Scandinavians, Finns, and Germans together to a dark and stinking coop in the forward hold of the ship. This disgusted us all for which reason we resisted going into the hold . . . I told the agent that I had a steerage ticket and I wouldn't go into that coop which wasn't fit for a man who murdered his own father. The agent said that it was the steerage advertised . . .

Other immigrants noted that on many liners the food was bad and too little was available, so that even a small amount of bad food could not be had except by crowding, vexation, and fighting. Not all recollections are so gloomy, however. Many immigrants noted that "when people got over the seasickness, there was plenty of dancing."

By the time Scandinavian emigration peaked, in the 1880s, larger liners sailing on regular schedules had taken over much of the emigrant traffic. These were faster, not so crowded, and altogether better geared for emigrants' needs. Not surprisingly, emigrants fared far better on these ships, with far fewer deaths.

With luck, the journey to the transatlantic ports would take only a few days, though sometimes weather or problems with the coastal vessels

would leave emigrants stranded in intermediate ports for days or even weeks. In the late 19th-century, the trip from the transatlantic ports averaged about 10 days, always depending on the state of the weather and the individual ship. At best, emigrants from Finland—the most distant Scandinavian country—might reach the United States in about two weeks in this period.

In the major ports, Scandinavians were joined by streams of emigrants from other European countries, all heading for America. Carrying with them prejudices of the old world, some Scandinavians objected to being packed "like sprats in salt" so closely with non-Scandinavians, especially Slavs from Eastern Europe. Enough Scandinavians felt that way for some liners to advertise that they carried only Scandinavian emigrants.

Scandinavians traveling steerage class experienced discrimination themselves. When a ship arrived in America, first-class passengers were let off at the main dock, after receiving only the briefest inspection on board. But steerage passengers were generally sent elsewhere, for a far more rigorous inspection, before they were let into the country.

Entering America

New York City was a main port of arrival, of course, and so were Boston and Philadelphia. Many immigrants went to Quebec, and on from there to cities in the upper Midwest or the prairie towns of Canada. But smaller ships might also use lesser ports, such as that at Portland, Maine.

Immigration inspections were carried out wherever new arrivals entered the country. But because so many people came through New York, stations were set up in the harbor for immigration inspection. From 1855 through most of the 19th century, immigrants entering the port of New York were processed at the foot of Manhattan at Castle Garden, once an old fort, later a musical theater, where Jenny Lind, the "Swedish Nightingale," sang in the 1850s. But from 1892 to 1897, and then again from 1900 to the 1930s, after rebuilding from a disastrous fire, immigrants were processed at a specially built station on Ellis Island, standing off the Statue of Liberty in New York Harbor.

Even though most Scandinavian immigrants in later times would be given a medical examination before leaving Europe, they were checked once more on arriving in the United States. Having crossed all the way from Scandinavia, some were at this point turned back, sometimes because of illnesses they had picked up on the journey. Certain diseases—such as the eye disease trachoma, which causes eventual blindness, and the highly contagious scalp disease called favus—were absolute bars to entry. The immigration service's medical inspectors also looked for many other diseases, such as heart problems, mental illness, or tuberculosis. If, in their opinion, the immigrant was likely to become a "public charge"—that is, to need welfare support—because of an illness, the unlucky traveler was

The shoreline around Castle Garden is being filled in here, just two years before the former fort would be opened as an immigration inspection station, in 1855. (Illustrated News, July 23, 1853)

On passing through Castle Garden into the streets of New York, many new immigrants were prey to thieves and swindlers. (Harper's Weekly, May 29, 1880, by A. B. Shults)

turned back at the gates of America.

In the late 19th century, immigrants needed little more than to pass the medical examination and to show the name and address of someone they were going to in the United States. That was especially true of Scandinavian immigrants, who were generally welcomed to America (as those from southern or eastern Europe were not).

But in the early 20th century, restrictions began to tighten. Working through interpreters, officials cross-examined immigrants on where they came from, what their background was, whether they had ever been in trouble with the law, and the like. Immigration officials—sometimes following regulations, but sometimes quite on their own—began to require immigrants to show a certain amount of money, generally $25, before allowing them to enter the country.

Immigrants also faced a peculiar problem. Even though many parts of the country were actively seeking immigrants to settle the land, labor organizations in industrialized areas feared that immigrants would take their jobs. So in 1885 they pushed through a contract labor act, forbidding recruitment of immigrants by American companies. Recruitment continued, of course. But immigrants had to tread a very fine line when speaking to the immigration inspectors. They could not say that they had firm jobs waiting for them—but they also could not say that they had no likelihood of work, since then they might be thought likely to become public charges. What they had to say was something like: "I have good prospects of work." But that was sometimes difficult for immigrants to understand and to convey through an interpreter. More than one party—like a group of nine Finns in 1892 who showed a letter asking them to come to Michigan to chop firewood—were turned back because they unwarily told of jobs waiting for them.

Far too many immigrants often arrived than could be processed in one day. Then, immigrants had to wait while questions were resolved or someone came to pick them up. In such cases, they were kept at the immigration station. In Castle Garden, they simply had to sleep where they could, on benches or on the floor; one Icelander in the 1870s advised his friends to bring soft bedding with them if they came through New York. At Ellis Island, sleeping provisions—hardly more satisfactory—consisted of bunks formed by wire mesh, three tiers high, with no bedding. It is no wonder that many immigrants said they were "made to sleep in cages." Some held aside for curable diseases were put in hospitals on Ellis Island.

Into the Country

Some immigrants stayed in or near the port cities where they first disembarked; New York at one time had the third largest concentration of Swedes in the country. But many immigrants were going far into the heartland, to the Midwest—to cities like Chicago, Milwaukee, or Madison—or even all the way to the Pacific coast.

In the early 19th century, many people traveled inland mostly on boats, via canals, rivers, and lakes. Immigrants generally took the standard route up the Hudson River, along the Erie Canal by packet boat—in tight quarters like "two mice in a mitten," one traveler said—and then on out through the Great Lakes. Later, when new railroad lines were carved through the Appalachian Mountains, immigrants more often went by train from New York across New Jersey to Philadelphia and Pittsburgh and on out to Chicago. From Illinois, they spread out through the upper Mississippi Valley and the western Great Lakes area, often taking riverboats at least partway to their destination.

But beyond the waterborne traffic, and in the years before the railroad was completed across the country in 1869, many immigrants traveled on foot. Those who could afford it had covered wagons drawn by teams of

In the early 19th century, many new immigrants traveled toward the Midwest in packet boats on the Erie Canal.
(Author's archives)

oxen, as shown in so many Western movies. But most of them simply walked, carrying their goods in a handcart, with four to six people responsible for pulling each cart.

Of course, railroad transportation would later ease the journey in both the United States and Canada. During the 1850s, for example, the Canadians opened a rail line direct from Quebec to Detroit, which was favored by many immigrants, especially Norwegians. Even so, many "immigrant trains" had literally been cattle cars, as proven by the continuing dirt and smell. They were slow, often being sent by roundabout routes, and had no sleeping or dining cars, even for week-long journeys far into the country.

Hazards in America

Much of America was so new and growing so fast that early immigrants had quite a difficult time getting to their destinations. Their problems were compounded by the fact that many of them spoke no English. Some were the targets of robbers; certainly their homespun or European-style country clothes marked them as "just off the boat." One Icelandic immigrant in the 1870s warned:

One must not become lost in daydreams on these travels for it is
essential in cities such as New York to take everything in at a glance,
and most important of all, to concentrate on where one is going.

Some never made it to their destinations at all, either because they were
persuaded by recruiters to go elsewhere, or because they were robbed or
misled and could not complete their journey. One group of Swedes arrived
at New York "without a penny" and looked for work to earn enough to get
them to Iowa. They were persuaded by a well-dressed Swedish gentleman
to follow him to jobs that, he said, were only three or four hours from
Iowa. Instead, they were taken to Richmond, Virginia, devastated at the
end of the Civil war, where they were "were treated almost like slaves."
The experience of such immigrants was not uncommon and spurred
efforts to shepherd newcomers more carefully on arrival.

Outright swindlers also operated on railroads and canal boats. Often
these were Scandinavians preying on their countrymen. In 1853 one
group of Norwegian immigrants met a "Norwegian rascal" who said he
was Pastor Ottesen of Manitowoc. He acted as their interpreter, gave them
milk, led them in prayers morning and night—then one day walked off
with most of their money. One young Swedish seaman, promised a fine job
for a lot of money, signed an English contract and handed over his money
to some new Swedish "friends"; he soon found that they had disappeared
and he had joined the army.

The government, too, began to watch over immigrants more carefully.
One of the main reasons for establishing the immigration station offshore
on Ellis Island was, in fact, to be better able to guard "greenhorns"—the
common name for new immigrants—from robbers and exploiters. Special
care was taken with single women because, in earlier years, some young
women were abandoned by their would-be husbands before marriage, or
were forced into prostitution. Immigrants heading inland would be
grouped by destination, with the train number marked on a label pinned to
their clothes.

Shipping lines and recruiters, too, took more care with travelers. Two
Finnish immigrants, Frans Lendén and Kustaa Grönfors, writing on
April 11, 1903, described the care taken on their journey:

The whole trip from Hanko on was led and shepherded so that you
could not escape except into the sea; if on land someone left the herd
by mistake then surely he was guided back; they feared that he would

get lost in a strange place; interpreters always met us where ever we touched land and commanded us . . . from the ship to the train and the train to the ship and "telekafi" or telegrams flowed on ahead so that a shepherd would be waiting to meet us at the station. So that no matter how much of a dunce you are you will surely be brought to the place on your ticket. . . .

Even so, not all immigrants reached their intended destinations—including those immigrants who had been recruited by American employment agents. Sometimes immigrants brought in to settle one area found jobs and land elsewhere more to their liking. The first group of Swedes brought in to settle in northeastern Maine, for example, was recruited to settle elsewhere. When the second group arrived, an agent guided them personally to their new home in Arostook County, prime potato country, where they founded "New Sweden," one of many communities so named around the country.

Unfortunately, in the early years not all immigrants had the money needed to take them across the country. That placed a heavy burden on those who tried to help newcomers. A dozen years after leading the first large Norwegian party to America, Lars Larsen Geilane was working in Rochester, New York, as a carpenter and shipbuilder. But his home was an unofficial way station for new immigrants, many of them Norwegian Quakers. Writing to a prominent Quaker in Norway, his wife lamented:

Twelve have arrived here today who are now eating their supper with us. About two weeks ago some ninety or a hundred persons came here. These stayed nearly a week's time in our and my brother's house, and we fed nearly all of them. . . . Most of them have now left for Illinois. . . . I will now ask you as a friend not to advise anyone to come who cannot get along on their own when they get here, for they nearly all come to us, and we cannot help so many. We do all we can. I have gone around town to find employment for them, and Lars has taken many of them out into the country.

For many, at the end of the journey was some unsettled, untenanted, almost untouched land out in the heart of the country. A Swedish immigrant named Hulda Belin, en route from Canada to the Midwest, captured the feeling of isolation that must have swept over the new immigrants:

So the train continued and we were in Michigan, U.S.A., and then into Minnesota's snowy wastes. The train made a stop and off of the train climbed a youth; he was tall and gangly, eighteen or nineteen years old, and you could see he was Swedish. Not a person was to be seen at the stop, that little square wooden house. He stood there alone and as though lost. He had no overcoat and it was cold. No one was in sight to meet him and no dwelling houses were to be seen. Then the train went on and he stood there alone. I have often wondered what his fate was.

So, in one way or another, in a city or on an unplowed plain, the immigrants reached the end of the journey—and the beginning of their life in the New World. While their journeys had many similarities, the members of each Scandinavian group had their own special experiences on their way to becoming Americans.

5

Swedish Immigrants in America

The first Swedes came to America as settlers in a group led by Peter Minuit, former Dutch governor of the New Netherlands. Several experienced Dutch traders had in the 1620s approached the Swedish king, Gustavus Adolphus, with tales of the riches to be gained in the New World. The king agreed to support a trading and settlement stock company, called the South Seas Company. Many Swedes bought stock in the company not only as a business investment, but also because they thought the company would do missionary work among the "heathens" of America. However, Gustavus Adolphus soon committed all of his resources to Europe's Protestant-Catholic conflict called the Thirty Years' War, in which he lost his life.

Peter Minuit then presented a similar plan to Count Axel Oxenstierna, chancellor during the infancy of Queen Christina, heir to the throne. Minuit had previously been dismissed by the Dutch, six years after he had purchased Manhattan, because he was dispensing Hudson River land grants too liberally. Despite this history, Oxenstierna approved of the planned expedition. Two ships left Stockholm on the last day of 1637 and arrived along the Delaware River—then called the South River—in March of 1638.

The Swedes settled along the Delaware River and Bay, from the southern cape, then called Paradise Point, to the Schuylkill River, which today flows through Philadelphia. The land had been purchased from the Native Americans for a colony: New Sweden. Among the early settlements was Fort Christina, named after the Swedish queen; this later became the city of Wilmington, Delaware. As more immigrants arrived over the next few years, the Swedes extended their settlements on the west side of the Delaware River, up to the falls of Trenton. Over 100 years later, descendants of these settlers are thought to have ferried Washington and his men across the Delaware. On the east side of the river they settled down as far south as Cape May, New Jersey.

But riches were not so easily come by. The first ship returning with goods from America carried stores worth only a little over half the expense of that first trip—and this ship never made it back to Sweden, but was lost at sea. Later ships had difficulty buying cargo from the other European colonies. Furs from the lands of New Sweden were not sufficient to bring the company, by then known as the Swedish Florida Company, into the black.

Wherever they settled, Swedish immigrants established churches, like this one, built in Wilmington, Delaware, in 1698. (Library of Congress, from *On Savage Shores*, by Edwin Markham, 1914)

But the Swedish settlers recognized the richness of the land and the value of the temperate climate. They convinced their government to furnish them with agricultural supplies and to buy out the disgruntled Dutch traders, who had no interest in farming. The Swedish government did so and sent the first Lutheran pastors, additional farm workers, and some skilled workers needed for permanent settlements. They also sent some Swedes and Finns convicted of minor offenses, such as default on debts, adultery, or burning timber—the traditional Finnish way of clearing the land, but against a just-passed Swedish law.

In 1643, the first Swedish governor, Johan Printz, arrived in New Sweden. He found a population of 135 men, 26 of whom died in the next year. The settlers were then increasingly left on their own by the Swedish government, which had troubles of its own in Europe. As the Swedes settled farther inland, they came into intense competition with both the English and the Dutch. The Dutch even built a fort downriver, outflanking and isolating one of the Swedish settlements. In 1653 Printz returned to Europe to plead for aid against these rival colonies.

While Printz was en route to the New World a relief boat was on its way to New Sweden. It carried 350 more immigrants, mostly in families. One hundred more had been left behind for lack of space on this, the last boatload of settlers to leave Sweden for over 180 years. The leader of the relief party, John Rising, ill-advisedly forced the southernmost Dutch settlement, Fort Casimir, to bow to him as governor in that area.

The Dutch were far from weak, however. Under Peter Stuyvesant, then governor of New Netherlands, they soon subdued the Swedes and gave them this choice: Any Swedes were free to return to Sweden, but those who stayed had to swear allegiance to the Dutch government. Only 37 chose to return.

The Swedish settlers who stayed were in time mostly forgotten by and lost to the Swedish nation. Lutheran pastors continued to be sent from Sweden to the area for over a century. But after that, the Swedes gradually blended into the general population in the Delaware River Valley. Later, when the Dutch lost control of the area, they became subjects of the British government. The last Swedish pastor of the Gloria Dei Church in Philadelphia died in 1831. When the later Swedish immigrants started arriving in the 1840s, few—if any—went to the Delaware River area expecting to find the descendants of the Swedish people who had settled in America 200 years before.

The settlers of New Sweden were the first European settlers in

Delaware and among the first in Pennsylvania, Maryland, and New Jersey. In the areas where they settled, they founded the first churches, put up the first buildings, cultivated the first land, built the first mills, and established Swedish governmental institutions. One especially notable contribution to American culture was the Swedish log cabin design. With its notched logs and corners chinked with clay, these cabins were used by settlers on the North American continent for hundreds of years.

Once Swedes had passed under Dutch and then British domination, they began to blend into the general "American" population. It was from Swedish settlers that William Penn later bought the land for his colony of Pennsylvania. Swedes were active in the local cultural and political organizations of the colonies, such as the American Philosophical Society founded by Benjamin Franklin in Philadelphia. How thoroughly they blended into the American mainstream is indicated by the fact that one of America's greatest presidents, whose name marks him as of Dutch descent also had an English and Swedish background: Franklin Delano Roosevelt.

People of Swedish descent were actively involved as America moved toward independence from Europe. A descendant of the original Swedish settlers, John Morton (born Mortenson), signed the Declaration of Independence. In fact, Morton—who also had Finnish and Norwegian ancestry—was carried on a litter from his sickbed to cast the deciding vote in favor of breaking with England. Another Swedish descendant was John Hanson, who was elected the "President of the United States in Congress Assembled" in 1781. That meant he was, in effect, the chief executive of the new nation during its first year. As such, he greeted George Washington on the general's first visit to Congress. He also led the fight to have the federal government, rather than the states, retain title to the "western lands." That allowed for the later formation of additional states of the union. During the actual War of Independence, Swedes along the Delaware were subjected to many hardships by the British troops for their support of the revolutionary cause.

From 1655 to 1840, few Swedish immigrants came to America. Those who did were often sailors, adventurers who had signed on board ship to see the world and decided to jump ship at an American port. One such ex-sailor was Svante Swenson, who arrived from Småland in 1836 and came to own thousands of acres of ranchland near Austin, Texas. Swenson brought in Swedish settlers under contract to help work the ranchland. These Swedes established a small permanent community near Austin,

John Hanson, a descendant of the earliest Swedish settlers, served as the first "President of the United States in Congress Assembled," in 1781-82, before George Washington was elected President of a new United States government.
(Library of Congress)

Texas, with their own churches and a Swedish paper, *Texas Posten*. The Swenson family was the first to fence off ranches in its area and brought the first Herefords to Texas. The climate was not to the liking of most Swedes, however, and few would later come to join the community, especially after the start of the Civil War.

The Main Migration

When the government lifted restrictions against emigration in the mid-19th century, Swedes generally tended to go to the Midwest. The sites of Swedish settlements in the United States are often the result of accident or of the decisions of a few individuals. One of the most important of these individuals was Gustav Unonius. A Swede born in Finland just after the territory was lost to Russia, Unonius had tried and dropped both military and medical careers. In 1840 he and his wife, with a dozen other well-to-do families, came to America as a romantic adventure.

Arriving in New York, they were surprised to find that they knew more about Illinois and Iowa than New Yorkers did. But some immigrants they met en route convinced them to go to Wisconsin. There they settled in a small community at Pine Lake, 30 miles west of Milwaukee. The land there looked beautiful in the summer, when they arrived. Writing in October of that year, Unonius lauded the region around Milwaukee.

> The soil here is the most fertile and wonderful that can be found and usually consists of rich black mold. Hunting and fishing will provide some food in the beginning, but they must be pursued sparingly, otherwise time which could more profitably be spent in cultivating the soil is wasted.

Unfortunately, Unonius and his party did not know that the winters there were much colder than in southern Sweden and that the land would be hard to farm. These immigrants were highly educated and not afraid of hard work, but they were entirely unsuited to a rough country life. Unonius and his wife lost four children in the wilderness. Eventually they moved to Chicago in 1849 and then back to Sweden in 1859. Others endured similar hardships. The Pine Lake community gradually scattered, with only a few remaining in the area.

Unonius, however, had an enormous impact on the future of Swedish migration. To earn extra money, he began to write "America letters," which were published in *Aftonbladet*, Sweden's popular afternoon newspaper. In the 1850s the Swedish novelist Frederika Bremer visited the United States, including the Pine Lake colony. She also wrote widely

Passing through Boston in 1852, this parade of early Swedish immigrants caught the attention of the city. (Library of Congress, *Gleason's Pictorial Drawing-Room Companion,* Rowse [Samuel Worcester])

circulated, favorable reports. As a result of reading these glowing reports of America, many Swedish immigrants came who were far better equipped to make their living from the land.

The first group of Swedes to settle in Iowa, for example, came to America because of letters they had read from one of the Pine Lake immigrants. This group of Lutherans, who settled in New Sweden, Iowa, did not flourish in the long run either. But they, too, wrote America letters.

Two groups attempting to join them did not complete their journey and, instead, founded new communities elsewhere. The first group followed the wrong fork of a river in Iowa. They became completely lost, ending up 200 miles from their destination. Some of the party retraced their steps to join those at New Sweden, but the rest stayed to found the town of Swede Point, later renamed Madrid, Iowa.

The second group heading for New Sweden had a terrible sea journey, during which several members died. Once in America and on their way to the Midwest, they were robbed while changing trains in Albany, New York. Their prepaid tickets took them only as far as Buffalo, New York, and they had no money to take them farther. Some found work near Buffalo and eventually made their way, not to Iowa, but to another Swedish settlement in Andover, Illinois. The rest eventually moved down to Jamestown, New York, and the area of Sugar Grove, just across the border in Pennsylvania. There, joined later by many skilled woodworkers from Småland, they established a major furniture-making center, with several large Swedish churches and, until World War II, a daily paper in Swedish.

The experience of these two groups was not uncommon and spurred the development of a support network for immigrants, with two brothers at the center. One brother, Olaf Hedstrom, arrived in New York as a sailor in the 1820s and was promptly robbed of all his funds. He was luckier than most—he had been trained as a sailor. He found a job, learned English, and along the way was converted to Methodism, working for a time as a circuit preacher in the Catskill Mountains, in upstate New York. Returning to Sweden to spread the word, Olaf converted his brother, Jonas, who joined him as a preacher in America. Jonas married a woman from the Catskills, and they followed her family west to Illinois. Olaf stayed in New York and became active in the Bethel Mission movement.

Between 1845 and 1875, a number of demasted ships were converted into chapels, which dispensed advice, Bibles, and occasionally money to weary, vulnerable immigrants arriving in New York harbor. These Bethel Missions helped Swedish immigrants to avoid the immediate dangers, such as being robbed, and to make the proper connections for their trip west. Olaf Hedstrom, preaching at the Bethel Mission, often advised immigrants to head toward Illinois. There his brother Jonas operated a virtual receiving station and settlement house. So it was that many thousands of Swedish immigrants found their way to Illinois.

Many of the Swedes who came in the 1840s and 1850s were groups of religious dissidents, unhappy with the repressive, state-supported Lutheran Church. One such group were the followers of Eric Janson, a Swedish revivalist preacher. Janson had called for a society of "lay readers"; he regarded religious books as unnecessary and even burned them. His followers, like members of other religious dissident groups in Sweden at the time, were often arrested for holding prayer meetings in their homes. The persecution became so severe that Janson and many of his followers decided to immigrate to America.

When Janson's advance scout arrived in New York City, he went to the Bethel Mission. There Olaf Hedstrom directed him toward Illinois. This was still in the early days of Illinois settlement—only 11 years after the first European had settled in Illinois and four years after Brigham Young and his Mormons had left Illinois for Utah.

The full Janson party arrived in Illinois in the fall of 1846. They named their new settlement Bishop Hill, after Janson's birthplace, Biskopskulla, near Uppsala, in Sweden. The site was too far from their more experienced neighbors, however, and the party was insufficiently prepared for the winter. Janson's followers first lived in tents, then dugouts—caves carved in the side of a hill—during the winter. Corn had to be ground by hand almost continually and was strictly rationed. More than that, no medical aid was available. By spring, so many had died that no boards were left for coffins; many were buried just in shrouds or mass graves. But once farming began in 1847, times were easier. Then more America letters went out across the sea. Between 1847 and 1854, almost 1,500 Swedes immigrated to Bishop Hill.

Dissatisfaction soon set in. The colony had been set as a communal religious society, in which members turned over all their goods to the community. Janson's power was complete and his rule became increasingly difficult to bear. At first he ordered celibacy, even in marriage; then he swung to the other extreme, ordering mass marriages of couples paired by him. Eventually Janson was assassinated by the husband of one of his members.

The Bishop Hill colony fell into disarray. Some members left to join nearby Methodist communities, such as Hedstrom's. Others followed gold rumors to California. The rest stayed, many of them forming Methodist churches in Bishop Hill. The Bishop Hill property was finally divided among the members in 1870.

This new wave of Swedish immigration had begun slowly. The 1850 census did not show large numbers of people of Swedish birth or parentage: Texas, 48; Illinois, 1123; Wisconsin 88; Iowa, 231; New York State, 753; Pennsylvania, 133. Other states showed even fewer. Only four Swedes were then shown as living in Minnesota. The first, Jacob Fahlstrom, had been a trader with the Hudson Bay Company, before marrying a Chippewa woman, Margaret Bungo, and settling down to farm in Minnesota. A panic in 1857 briefly slowed even this small amount of migration, as some Swedes returned to Europe.

Then in the 1860s the Civil War first disrupted immigration and also changed its character. In those troubled times, fewer families emigrated, but many more single men rushed to America. Some who had embarked on military careers in neutral Sweden came to gain practical experience in action with the Union forces. They often served as officers in the war and then returned to Sweden to continue their careers.

Many other young men, however, were unofficially but actively recruited for the Union army. Some joined, while others worked as support laborers, such as blacksmiths and carpenters, in this fast-growing land that always had need of skilled people. Many of these wartime immigrants stayed in America and later moved west to settle land that was being opened for development.

In this period many land and railroad companies and state governments began to employ agents to recruit immigrants to clear and settle undeveloped land. One state that carried on an active recruitment program was Minnesota. The results are clear. In 1860, Minnesota had only 3,178 residents of Swedish birth or parentage. By 1870, that number had increased to almost 21,000; by 1900 it was over 100,000. Michigan, Wisconsin, Indiana, as well as Illinois and Iowa, also benefited from this increased recruitment.

Meanwhile immigration conditions were changing. Shipping lines were building ships better suited for travelers, and they were advertising for passengers. So more and more immigrants began to travel alone or in small parties, often to join friends or family already in America. That, too, came to be a selling point for land promoters. They would arrange for new immigrants to buy prepaid tickets, sometimes at discounts, to bring over others from Europe to join them.

All of these moves had their effect. Swedish immigration reached its peak in 1882, when 65,000 Swedes came to the United States. In 1888, the number peaked again at almost 55,000. Between 1815 and 1900 the total number of Swedish immigrants was about 850,000.

The New Life

Like all pioneers, those Swedish immigrants who opened the western wilderness areas often had to live in primitive conditions. Like Janson's party at Bishop Hill, they had to live in tents or dugouts until they could build log cabins. Clothing was homemade and shoes often wooden. Food consisted mostly of Indian corn or wheat and vegetables, supplemented by milk, fish, and pork when available. In isolated areas, a farmer might have to walk 40 or 50 miles to the nearest mill. As the Swedish families settled in, however, and became more prosperous, they adopted general American styles of dress and housing.

In the opening up of the western lands, Swedes cleared for cultivation as much land as any other ethnic group in the United States, perhaps more—over 10,000,000 acres, with over 2,000,000 acres in Minnesota alone. Their move westward was closely intertwined with the westward push of the railroads. Between 1850 and 1890, many Swedes worked to build railroads such as the Rock Island Line in Illinois and the Northern Pacific lines through Minnesota and North Dakota. Then they stayed to become farmers and build new towns in areas made newly accessible by these railroads.

Politics and War

Swedes have always been politically active, especially on the local level, where they were the main ethnic group in many of the isolated towns and counties they founded. In Illinois, which had the largest number of Swedes in the Union in the 19th century, Swedes were extremely interested in the Lincoln-Douglas debates. Because they believed slavery to be morally wrong, they actively supported Lincoln. The 80 Swedish voters of Rockford, Illinois, are said to have gone to the polls as a body under their pastor, to vote for Lincoln. In the Civil War, one out of five members of the Swedish population in Illinois volunteered to fight. (For the state as a whole, by contrast, the figures were one out of seven.) Many Union companies were mostly Scandinavian and one, from Bishop Hill, was entirely Swedish.

Relatively few Swedes had settled in the South, partly because the warm climate was not to their taste, and partly because of their strong feelings about slavery. As a result, few Swedish immigrants fought on the Confederate side. However, the Bishop Hill company placed a Swede in charge of the Confederate artillery at the battle of Shiloh. (That company later accompanied Union General Sherman on his march "from Atlanta to the sea.")

Because of their education and military experience, many Swedes became officers. One, Charles Stolbrand, was commissioned a brigadier general by Lincoln. Stolbrand, who had been the head of the Svea Society in Chicago before the war, settled in South Carolina after the war and became active in real estate and politics there. Two other Swedes who made important contributions to the war were Captain John Ericsson, who designed the Union ironclad, *Monitor*, and Admiral John Dahlgren, who designed its guns.

Swedish-American John Ericsson designed the ironclad ship, the Monitor *used by the Union navy in the Civil War.*
(Library of Congress)

Many officers returned from the Civil War to popular acclaim, which helped build their careers. One such veteran, Colonel Hans Mattson, was employed by the Minnesota State Board of Immigration to promote Minnesota to potential settlers. His success led to his being elected Secretary of State of Minnesota. Later he was appointed American consul to Calcutta, India, by President Garfield. Minnesota came to have the largest proportion of Swedes and by the mid-20th century the largest number of Swedish-Americans altogether. The first Swedish governors were all from Minnesota.

Religion and Education

Swedes have always been a religious people, though with some disagreements on the form of worship. While many of the earliest Swedish immigrants in the 19th century were religious dissidents, the large majority of Swedish-Americans are and have been Lutherans.

Churches serving the early Swedish-born populations generally held their services in Swedish. "Vacation schools" were commonly set up for the children, sometimes during the summer but occasionally all year round. Supplementing regular public schools, these vacation schools taught Swedish, the catechism, and church history.

Immigrants, like these two Swedish children, often arrived in America wearing their best clothes in the old country style.
(National Park Service, by Augustus Francis Sherman)

(Later generations came to reject the Swedish language—some even left the church over the language issue.) Gradually churches came to use English primarily. By degrees the separate Swedish or Scandinavian branches of the various churches, such as Lutheran or Methodist, dropped the designation "Swedish" and merged with the mainstream American church organizations.

Swedes are a highly literate people. Valuing education as they did, the first institution they established, after a church, was usually a school. In isolated areas, the schools at first taught in Swedish. (One notable exception was the Bishop Hill community, where Eric Janson early saw the need for everyone to know English.) Swedes protested against the laws that, in many states, required a school to teach in English, if it was to be officially recognized. In practice, however, as areas became more heavily settled, schools came to teach in English.

(This laid the basis for many second and third generation Swedish-Americans—the children and grandchildren of immigrants—to move into higher education, and from there into white collar and professional work. The combination of religious fervor and respect for higher education led Swedes (sometimes joined by other Scandinavians) to establish many church-related colleges and seminaries. Among the best known of these schools are Bethany College in Lindsborg, Kansas; Augustana College at Rock Island, Illinois; Gustavus Adolphus College in St. Peter, Minnesota; and Upsala College in East Orange, New Jersey. The Illinois State University at Springfield, Illinois, was also originally a Lutheran seminary.

Swedish-American Culture

Swedish feeling for religion and learning also combined in the many Swedish-language publications. Well over 1,200 Swedish-language periodicals, most of them short-lived, have existed since the 1840s, over 100 in Chicago alone. Only half a dozen survived into the 1970s. Swedes also established a Swedish-language publishing house, the Augustana. Most of these publications gradually shifted from a wholly religious focus to become more political or general. The first fully secular Swedish newspaper, *Svenska Amerikanaren*, was started in Chicago in 1866.

Such newspapers regularly reported news of Sweden, with correspondence and summaries of events from the homeland, as well as

news on local conditions, such as crop outlooks and market prices. They
also published in serial form, on pullout pages that could be folded and
kept, the works of great Swedish writers and of English or American
writers translated into Swedish.

These papers formed an important, continuing contact with the home
country. They often generated considerable relief money for victims of
catastrophe in Sweden. For example, during the 1902-1903 famine in
northern Sweden, the Minneapolis paper *Svenska Amerikanska* alone sent
$18,000 in relief funds to Sweden.

Swedes also kept alive their heritage through various organizations.
Some were general fraternal and insurance societies, set up for social and
mutual benefits. Among the largest fraternal groups to last into the 20th
century are the Vasa Order of America and the Scandinavian Fraternity of
America. Others were set up in a particular region, such as the United
Swedish Societies of Greater New York, and the Svea Society in Chicago.

Still others focused on mutual interests, such as the American Union of Swedish Engineers or the American Union of Swedish Singers. Across the country Swedes founded countless singing groups and gymnastics societies.

Swedish immigration was cut sharply during World War I, but rose again somewhat after the war, when the United States experienced a boom, while Sweden was in a mild depression. Even so, emigration from Sweden was never more than 19,000 a year after the war. By this period almost three-quarters of the immigrants were single young men and women, come to make it in the New World on their own. But once the Great Depression hit, immigration fell off sharply. The Swedish immigration quota, set in 1924 as part of a general immigration restriction, was never filled.

Swedish-American Charles A. Lindbergh, Jr., made aviation history by sailing solo in his airplane, "The Spirit of St. Louis," across the Atlantic from America to Europe. (Library of Congress)

6

Norwegian Immigrants in America

Here it is not asked, what or who was your father, but the question is, what are you?

From an America letter by a
19th-century Norwegian immigrant

No country, except Ireland, has sent such a large proportion of its population to America as Norway. Nearly one million Norwegians immigrated to America between the 1820s and the 1920s. Since the whole population of Norway in 1820 was still under one million, this was clearly a century of rapidly rising population.

The earliest Norwegian immigrants to America came by way of the Netherlands. In the 17th century, some sailors and others migrated to Amsterdam and other Dutch cities in search of work. Some of these then made their way with the Dutch to the city of New Amsterdam (renamed New York in 1663). Since Norway was, at that time, a province of Denmark, some Norwegians immigrated to the Danish West Indies (Virgin Islands), generally as sailors, clerks, or officials. From there, some came eventually to the mainland of North America. Some Norwegians who had converted to the Moravian form of Protestantism, joined and merged with German Moravian communities in Pennsylvania in the mid-18th century.

A few other Norwegians also found a route to North America. At least one is celebrated in a monument from the War of 1812. A 23-year-old Norwegian carpenter named John David arrived in California in 1828, when it was still part of Mexico. He had come by way of the Sandwich Islands in the Pacific Ocean and settled in Los Angeles. Another Norwegian sailor, Peter Storm, arrived in California in around 1830. It is said that he painted the flag in 1846 for the short-lived "Bear Flag Revolt," when some United States citizens proclaimed California—then Mexican territory—an independent republic.

The Sloopers

But until the early 19th century, the number of Norwegians in the United States was very small. Then, in the summer of 1825—on the appropriate date of July 4th—the first fair-sized group of Norwegians left Norway for America. A party of 52, 10 of them married couples and many of them children (an additional child was born on board ship), left the port of Stavanger in a sloop called *Restaurationen*, a name partly Americanized to *Restauration*. Norwegian historian Ingrid Semmingsen called the *Restauration* "a mere nutshell of a vessel," with only one-quarter the carrying capacity of the *Mayflower*. But these 52 brave souls had apparently pooled most of their money to buy the ship and enough provisions for three months. Their plan was to sell the sloop on their arrival in New York, and thus get the funds needed for settling in the New World.

The *Restauration* did not head directly for the New World. After putting in at a small English port, the travelers sold illegal brandy to the local inhabitants. Moving on, they plucked out of the English Channel a barrel of Madeira wine. They proceeded to drink so much of it that, we are told, they drifted into a Spanish port almost without guidance, "just like a pest [plague] ship." The Norwegian-Swedish consul there checked their papers and, after they had reprovisioned, they went on their way. The voyage of the tiny sloop took three months. It arrived in New York on October 9, 1825. One local paper, the *New York Daily Advertiser*, reported the event, describing the farmers of the party as wearing plain homespun clothing, while the city dwellers were dressed in bright calicoes, ginghams, and colored shawls, probably imported from England. The reporter was astonished that they had arrived safely, for he did not consider the ship safe for the voyage.

The size of the ship caused a different problem, for the American government had in 1819 passed a law stating that for every five tons—meaning tonnage of water it displaced—a ship could carry only two people. Since the *Restauration* carried far too many people, it was subject to fines amounting to $3,000—an enormous amount in those days. But a prominent Quaker from New York helped them, obtaining a waiver of the fine from President John Quincy Adams on November 5.

Unfortunately, the immigrants got a price of only $400 for the *Restauration*, much less than they had expected. But with help from the local Quakers they were able to complete their journey to northern New York State, in Kendall Township, on the shores of Lake Ontario.

That the Quakers helped these immigrants was not surprising. Many of the immigrants themselves were apparently Quakers, or at least Quaker sympathizers. Few of them had openly belonged to Quaker congregations—called Societies of Friends—in Norway. But once in America, where they could worship freely as they chose, many became Quakers. Some others were followers of the Norwegian religious leader Hans Nielsen Hauge, whose beliefs were much like those of the Quakers. The rest of the immigrants joined other religious groups once in the United States, and a few remained Lutheran—though with much more freedom, since there was no state church.

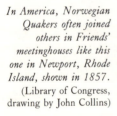

In America, Norwegian Quakers often joined others in Friends' meetinghouses like this one in Newport, Rhode Island, shown in 1857. (Library of Congress, drawing by John Collins)

These Norwegian immigrants—their descendants call themselves "sloopers"—were the pioneers of Norwegian immigration. Their first years were very hard. Most of the immigrants were able to earn money only from odd jobs and required charity from their neighbors to survive. Almost no one in the party spoke English, and they were at first inclined to keep to themselves, holding to their old Norwegian ways. One man, English-speaking Cleng Peerson (born Kleng Pedersen Hesthammer), was apparently the sloopers' main go-between with their non-Norwegian neighbors. He had been their advance scout, selecting the Kendall site on an 1821 trip to the United States.

Because the adjustment period was long and difficult, few other immigrants followed to join the settlers in Kendall for the first years. But the adjustment was necessary for, even if they had had enough money to take them back to Norway, they would have arrived as paupers. By the 1830s, however, most immigrants had begun to know their neighbors and to earn enough money to support themselves reasonably well.

Though they did not know it at the time, these sloopers were also placed along one of the main pathways to the heart of the continent. In 1825, the year they arrived, New Yorkers had opened the Erie Canal, linking the Hudson and Mohawk rivers with the Great Lakes and the whole Middle West. By the 1830s large numbers of European immigrants, as well as Americans from east of the Appalachian Mountains, were heading westward on this route to places in Ohio and farther on to what were then the small towns of Chicago and Milwaukee. Many of them traveled by canal barges, but others went overland, for this was the easiest level route to the American West, north of Georgia.

Some of the sloopers, interested by tales of the western lands, went to explore for themselves. Fifty-year-old Cleng Peerson—who had traveled widely in the world as a sailor and had the important advantage of being able to speak English—headed west on foot in 1833. Through Ohio and Indiana he went, until at last he came to Illinois. That was, to him, the "Promised Land"—and at only $1.25 per acre. Peerson found the land so beautiful and described it so eloquently that within a few years most of the Kendall sloopers had followed him. They sold their land in New York at a modest profit—partly because of the Erie Canal—and settled in the valley of the Fox River in northern Illinois, about 60 miles southwest of Chicago.

Once happily settled in Illinois, the sloopers began to write the traditional "America letters" back home. Most influential of these writers was Gjert Gregoriussen Hovland, who arrived in Kendall in 1831. He talked of religious and economic freedom, of social equality, of "beautiful and fertile soil," of "employment and a livelihood for anyone who is willing to work," and of laws that worked for "the common man's well-being and advantage."

In the 1830s, with some poor harvests and widespread famine in Norway, these letters caused a sensation. Many were copied by hand and circulated in small communities scattered around Norway. The occasional Norwegian-American back home for a visit—a rare, expensive, but not unheard-of-trip—drew people from miles around, all of whom wished to hear about the new land.

New Immigrants

There was so much interest that the Kohler shipping firm decided to outfit two brigs for the emigrant journey. In 1836, the vessels left for America with 167 emigrants on board, mostly peasant families. These were, according to one of the captains, "quiet, well-behaved people, who wore their best clothes and had a good coloring." Many of them, too, had Quaker connections and were greeted by large numbers of fellow Quakers on their arrival in New York.

Once started, the stream of Norwegian immigrants continued to flow. Many of them followed Cleng Peerson's lead out to Illinois. Peerson himself, ever a wanderer, later went on to Missouri and Iowa, then back to join a Swedish commune at Bishop Hill, and finally to a Norwegian community in Texas, where he died at the age of 82.

The community in Texas was the only successful Norwegian settlement in the South. Most of the immigrants who followed Peerson settled north and west of Illinois. They still generally traveled in large groups, though some individuals made their way to the United States. After the 1840s, the center of Norwegian settlement shifted from Illinois to Wisconsin, near Lake Muskego in Waukesha County and Lake Koshkonong in Dane County, and in communities like Jefferson Prairie in Rock County.

A surprising number of these early Norwegian immigrants were mature people in their fifties and even sixties. Some of them had been quite active in Norway's political life, which was changing fast enough to permit them to dissent, but not fast enough for people who saw full freedom across the ocean. The majority were younger couples, perhaps 35 to 40 years old, often with large families. As always, some were single men. A rare few were single women on their own.

Elise Tvede, for example, had in 1846 become editor of a periodical called *Norway and America*, devoted to news about Norwegian immigrants in America. A year later she herself emigrated, joining a small Norwegian community not far from Dallas, Texas, remarrying there. (She and her first husband had divorced in Norway, a rare occurrence at the time.) Elise Tvede Waerenskjold became a proud defender of Texas, writing a history of its first Norwegian community, and continued the temperance activities she had started in Norway, as well as founding a reading circle to bring culture to the area.

As in all ethnic groups, Norwegians came in chains of immigrants. One young woman from Bergen came to Boston because she had married an American sailor. Her brother, Peder Anderson, followed her and settled in nearby Lowell, Massachusetts. As Peder became a successful industrialist, he brought to America most of their family.

And, of course, being largely a sailing people, many Norwegians were to be found in the port cities of America. One Norwegian-American wrote in 1837 that when a Norwegian arrived in New York, he needed only to call out a phrase in Norwegian to find one of his countrymen to talk with.

Many of these early immigrants were skilled and sometimes highly educated people. They at least had the considerable amount of money required to pay their way across the ocean. Poorer people, sometimes a single man or woman, or a young couple, could sometimes arrange to have someone pay for their passage, in return for work in America. Others received money for their fares from those who had gone to America earlier. In general the Norwegian immigrants were among the best and the brightest people of their time and place. Vilhelm Moberg, in his novel *The Emigrants*, put it this way:

> It was the boldest who first set off. The enterprising ones made the decision. The venturesome ones started out first on the journey across the great sea. They were the dissatisfied ones and the initiators who could not endure their lot at home and who became the first emigrants in their community.

Not all of the Norwegian communities in the new land were successful. A community of Norwegians, followers of the Moravian religion, settled near Green Bay, Wisconsin, in about 1850. Like many early

Scandinavian settlements, this one was intended as a utopia. Everything was to be owned and worked in common. Unfortunately, class divisions disrupted the harmony of the community. The settlers distrusted the leader, Nils Otto Tank, who had bought the land originally and given it to the whole community. Because Tank came from a wealthy landed family, the settlers feared they would become simply his poor workers. So gradually they moved away, a little north, where they bought their own land individually.

One settlement, founded in 1837 in Beaver Creek, Illinois, was particularly unhappy. The land the party had selected was marshy and malaria-ridden. Within a few years, most of the group, including the leader, Ole Rynning, was dead. The rest left the ill-fated settlement behind and headed for greener pastures. But before he died, Rynning wrote a book called *True Account about America for the Information and Help of Peasant and Commoner*, believing that immigrants should know as much as possible about the new land before deciding to set out on the journey. Like the America letters, Rynning's book—despite its attempt to present both the positive and negative aspects of America—attracted many new immigrants.

Precisely how many people came from Norway to America in the mid-19th century is not clear. Local pastors were supposed to record everyone who moved out of their parish, and the government was supposed to issue

Norwegian immigrants in wooded country often lived in log cabins like this, surrounded by the stumps of trees they had felled.
(Norsk Folkemuseum)

passports to everyone who left the country. In fact, the records were kept haphazardly. Until about 1843, a few hundred emigrants left each year. But by 1843, the figure was up to 1,600. (It would not drop below 1,000 until 1930, after the start of the great worldwide Depression.) After that it varied, higher when Norway was in depression, lower when America was at war or in its own depression. Altogether, 17,000 to 18,000 Norwegians had arrived in the United States by the end of 1850. These people were primarily from high in the mountains or deep inland at the heads of fjords, more than from the lowlands, whose population was more likely to migrate to one of Norway's cities than to go abroad.

Evidence of America's opportunity was perhaps best seen by the success of some of these very poor emigrants. In village after village, America's riches were confirmed by a trickle and later a stream of money and tickets sent back by emigrants to help others follow them. A Norwegian pastor, writing in the late 1850s, told of "a cotter's son, who was so poor at the time of his emigration that I married him free of charge, sent a draft of 400 specie [hard coin] dollars . . . to his father and his siblings so that they could join him."

Lure of the West

The discovery of gold in California in 1848 attracted Norwegians from the other side of the world, and helped change the character of Norwegian immigration. While most Norwegian immigrants in the early 19th century were mature people with families, after the gold fever of 1849 many more were young, unmarried men. Some of these were seemingly quite unsuited for their adventurous life, being young men who had previously "lived a fashionable hotel and café life at the expense of their parents." Many came to be lifelong gold-seekers, sailing off to Australia, British Columbia, later Alaska, at the first reports of gold strikes. Others were drawn to the Pacific Northwest, so much like their own homeland, and became the first Norwegians to settle in Oregon and Washington.

Many stayed right in California, later forsaking the gold fields for other lines of work. By 1860, there were some 700 Norwegian immigrants in California, many of them living near the wharves in San Francisco. Johan Nordtvedt, who changed his name to John G. North, became a shipbuilder there. Peder Saeter—later changed to Peter

Sather—became a rich banker, who made many contributions to the University of California at Berkeley.

But perhaps the best-known Norwegian in California was John Thoresen Rue, who introduced skiing to California. He used skis for 20 years on his mail route through the Sierra Nevada Mountains in the mid-19th century, carving out the route later followed by the Central Pacific Railroad. Because skis were unknown in the region, Californians called them "Norwegian Snowshoes," giving him the nickname "Snowshoe Thompson."

Gold fever also affected Norwegians from the Midwest, and set many of them on the overland route to the West coast. The *Nordlyset* of Rochester and Racine, Wisconsin, for example, wrote in January 1849: "No pen can describe the excitement that runs through all classes of citizens." By March, they were reporting: "The gold fever rages with frightful intensity among us at present. A number of emigrants have recently returned with the seed of the illness in their pockets, and the contagion has spread near and far. High and low, rich and poor—they have been attacked together." By November 1849 the paper was having a hard time keeping up publication, for all its typographers had left for California.

Some people left their homes and families behind when they went to California. Some returned disappointed and poorer than when they had left. And some of those who did make modest gains in California, did not even make it home with them. A Norwegian-American named Nielsen, from Rock Run, Illinois, lost $1,350 in gold during a riot in Panama.

But many Norwegian-American families sold their farms and, in small parties, joined the great stream of covered wagons out across the Great Plains and the Rockies to California. They were to be pathfinders in a secondary migration, which would bring many Norwegian-Americans to the Pacific Coast, long after the gold fever had subsided. Not all the pathfinders were gold-seekers, though. Some Norwegian Mormons had, after 1847, joined the Mormon exodus to Salt Lake City, Utah.

This new emigration was much like the first. A relatively few adventurous souls headed west to scout the new land. They sent back letters to their friends and families in the Midwest, which were often published in local Norwegian-American papers as "Letters to the Editor" *(Breve fra folket)*. These described the land, the crops, the weather, the economic opportunity, the social and religious life—just as early America letters had described the Midwest to Norway. Norwegians, and other Scandinavians as well, read these letters, talked about them endlessly, and sometimes took to the trails to join their kinfolk on the Pacific Coast.

One of the main attractions of the Pacific Coast, especially the Northwest, was its similarity to life at home in Norway. Many of those who left for the Pacific Coast, especially for the Northwest, had been unhappy with the Midwest, since it was so different from their homeland. Coming to the Midwest had involved great adjustments, and not everyone had made them successfully.

This had been the pattern: Those who arrived in the Midwest with little money of their own generally started out working as hired laborers on farms owned by others. In one or two years, they could earn enough to buy a team of animals and the necessary tools. Then they would become tenant farmers, working land rented from others. The next step was to buy their own land. Over the years, as more and more people moved into the Midwest, land became more expensive and somewhat more scarce. Then, when it came time to buy their own land, many of these settlers moved on to Iowa, and the open prairies of Minnesota and the Dakotas.

All of this was a very big change for the Norwegian immigrants. In the old country, they had pieced together a living, from small-scale farming, a little logging, some fishing, occasional sailing trips, and handcrafts in the winter. But in the United States, many worked very large corn and wheat farms, or cattle ranches—a far cry from the meager plots they had left behind. The adjustment to the new type of farming was difficult, and not everyone was happy with it.

But the Pacific Northwest was like the old country in many ways—cool, tree-covered, near the sea. And the pattern there was to farm small plots, not the huge Midwest acreage. So, for many, going to the Pacific Northwest was like going back home to the old country, but with a new freedom and opportunity.

From the 1880s on, many new emigrants from Norway went directly to the Pacific Coast, to Oregon, Washington (especially around Seattle and the Puget Sound), and Alaska—as well as to Canada's British Columbia between the two. These were often skilled crafts people and sailors, who put their skills to work in the forests and on the rivers and oceans of their new land.

In the same period, many Norwegians came to settle on the East Coast, as well. Many were sailors who jumped ship, often in New York, in the old-fashioned pattern of immigration. Between 1875 and 1885, perhaps as many as 800 sailors entered the United States in this way. Many of them stayed in the coastal cities, working on ships or docks, piers or shipyards. They formed the nucleus of a substantial Norwegian community in Brooklyn.

Norwegian-American Culture

In the farflung regions to which they had dispersed, and even in the Midwestern states where they had large populations, Norwegians often formed close ties with other Northern European groups. In the Midwest, they often formed their own Norwegian churches. Like other Scandinavians, they had sharp religious disagreements, and a single Norwegian community might have several different churches—generally Lutheran, but also Methodist, Baptist, Mormon, and other Protestant groups. But in Midwestern areas just being opened to settlement, and in the coastal states, where they were rather spread out, Norwegians were often joined by German neighbors in their churches, or by Icelanders or Danes, whose numbers were smaller. In such areas, Norwegians often both gave and received help from their fellow settlers. They were, for example, especially helpful to the earliest Icelandic settlers.

Like the Swedes in newly opened parts of the Midwest, Norwegians at first resisted the public schools taught in English. They wanted to hold to their own language, but more than that, they were dissatisfied with the quality of the crude frontier schools. They organized summer schools, Sunday schools, and even alternative parochial schools, taught wholly or partly in Norwegian.

Norwegians also established a number of colleges, many of them originally to train ministers. The first such Norwegian seminary was Luther College, in Decorah, Iowa, in 1865. The largest college, which developed into a full liberal arts institution, was St. Olaf College in Northfield, Minnesota. Norwegians, sometimes in partnership with Swedes or Danes, founded several other colleges as well, including Augsburg College, in Minneapolis, Minnesota; Augustana College, in Sioux Falls, South Dakota; Concordia College, in Moorhead, Minnesota; and Pacific Lutheran College, in Parkland, Washington. These kept alive Norwegian culture and traditions among the younger generations, even though in later times Norwegian was taught as a "foreign" language, and

New settlers built schoolhouses to ensure that their children received a proper education. This is the Lade Farm school in Fosston, Minnesota. (Minnesota Historical Society)

English was the main language of education.

Norwegians also formed many social clubs and fraternities, sometimes with other Scandinavians. Many of these were mutual benefit or charity organizations, designed to help immigrants through rough periods. The Sons of Norway, today primarily a network of social clubs, started out as just such a mutual-insurance group. Many others were more purely cultural—literary, dramatic, or choral groups of all sorts. In the late 19th century, the United Scandinavian Singers of America, in which the Norwegians played a prominent part, held musical festivals every other year. Such cooperation ended for many groups in the early 20th century, when Norway and Sweden were dissolving their union in Europe. This group, for example, then became the Norwegian Singers' Association, with more than 40 clubs in the 1930s.

Norwegians also formed a special kind of group: the *bygdelag*. These were organizations for people from the same region (*bygd*) in Norway. The first of these was Valdres Samband (Valdres Association), founded for people from the Valdres Valley in 1902 by Andrew A. Veblen, college professor and brother of the world-renowned economist Thorstein Veblen.

Many other *bygdelags* followed. These groups kept genealogies and archives, holding meetings and festivals to keep alive the culture of their native region. Many *bygdelags* later banded together in a Joint Council. In 1925 they held a four-day celebration—for which they built a full-scale model of the *Restauration*—in Minneapolis to honor the centennial of Norwegian immigration to that city.

Though Norwegians were spread widely around the country, the press helped keep them in touch with each other. A weekly *Nordlyset* (*Northern Lights*) was founded in Muskego, Wisconsin, in 1847. It was soon followed by a stream of papers, among them the *Emigranten*, also in Wisconsin, *Faedrelandet* (*Fatherland*), *Budstikken* (*Messenger*), *Minneapolis Tidende* (*Minneapolis Times*), *Decorah-Posten*, and *Western Viking* of Seattle. Over the decades these six papers merged in the order listed above, as the Norwegian-speaking audience shrank, and gradually moved toward use of English. They published a great many Norwegian immigrant writers. Norwegians also had a succession of smaller papers on labor issues, some edited by the reformer Marcus Thrane, once imprisoned in his homeland for his reform activities.

Like the Swedes, Norwegians were strongly against slavery. Though some in the early 19th century had been Democrats, the majority of Norwegian-Americans joined the Republican Party in the 1850s, largely because of its antislavery platform. One group of Norwegian-American Lutheran pastors even cut their connection with a larger church organization based in St. Louis, because they thought it favored slavery.

As Norwegians moved into political office, many of them were Republicans, such as Knute Nelson, governor and later U.S. senator from Minnesota. Later, however, many of them became unhappy with the big business leanings of the Republicans and instead joined progressive parties more devoted to "the common man," such as the Farmers' Alliance and the Populist Party.

Norwegian immigration began to slow markedly in the mid-1920s, so it never filled the quota set by the U.S. Immigration Service in 1924. By the mid-1940s only about 2,000 Norwegians a year came to the United States, a figure that has been dropping ever since.

7

Finnish Immigrants in America

The first Finns arrived in America in the middle of the 17th century. In the Delaware River region, some 500 Finns joined the colony of New Sweden between its founding in 1638 and its conquest by the Dutch in 1655. These were some of the 4,000 Finns who, over some decades, had crossed the Gulf of Bothnia by invitation to settle some wilderness parts of southwestern Sweden. They had run afoul of a Swedish law against burning woodlands—the typical Finnish method of clearing land for farming. Given a choice of prison or emigration, these Finns—called "burnbeaters"—chose the New World.

These Finnish-Americans helped open the lands of Delaware, Maryland, and Pennsylvania, establishing the early patterns of settlement there. But once these regions were taken by the Dutch, many Finns moved to the New Jersey side of the Delaware River, at places like Finns Point (near Salem). Later, when the English took over, the Finns—like their fellow Swedish colonists—gradually became absorbed in the general "American" population, over the decades adopting the dominant language of English and taking Anglicized names. But not without protest. In 1669, an aristocratic Swede-Finn settler, nicknamed "The Long Finn," led a rebellion against English rule, but to no avail. John Morton (born Mortenson), who signed the Declaration of Independence, was of mixed Swedish-Finnish-Norwegian descent. Ties with the homeland were gradually lost and, within a century, no Swedish- or Finnish-speaking families could be found in the area. Only a few hints of Finnish background remained, especially around Chester, Pennsylvania, at one time called Finland.

The Early 19th-Century Migration

Between the 1600s and the mid-19th century only a few Finns made their way to America. Most of these were sailors, who arrived in American ports, liked what they saw, and decided to stay. How many, who they were, and where they settled is not at all clear. We know of one Finn, William Lundell, who became a farmer in Massachusetts in around 1830. In 1833 a Finnish sailor named Carl Sjödahl arrived in the United States; under the name Charles Linn he became a rich man in Alabama.

In the early 19th century, some Finns went to Alaska, since both it and Finland were then held by the Russians. Like the Russian colonists they joined, these Finns generally lived by fishing, whaling, or fur trapping. Two, however, served as governors of Alaska, including Arvid A. Etholen, in the early 1840s. Alaskan Finns are credited with building the first Protestant church on North America's Pacific Coast, in Sitka in the 1840s, perhaps even earlier. Finns remained prominent in Alaska after it was bought by the United States in 1867. Some of them did return to Finland at that point, while others immigrated to Canada or to the United States mainland. But after the 1880s, with the discovery of gold in Alaska, they would be joined by many other Finnish immigrants, especially in Sitka, Juneau, Fairbanks, and Anchorage.

Until the 1860s, most Finnish immigrants were still sailors. After 1849, with the discovery of gold in California, many Finnish sailors—like their fellow mariners from other parts of the world—jumped ship in American ports and made their way by land or sea to California. Some from Russian ships were also trying to avoid being pressed into service in the Crimean War in 1854. Some, by contrast, were successfully recruited to join the Union navy during America's Civil War. Sailors continued to immigrate in just this way throughout the 19th century and even up to the beginning of World War I.

The Main Migration

With gold fever in the air, however, some other Finns began to apply to the Finnish government for passports to go to America. One of the first of these legal entrants was Edvard Kohn of Turku. Soon others began to emigrate from the coastal towns, largely individuals or families who had had to leave the land and had recently come to the city in search of work. By the 1860s, Finns had begun to arrive in some numbers from the Bothnian regions around Vaasa and Oulu, first from the coastal areas, then from inland.

By the early 1860s, there were probably several hundred Finns in America. Some of these later returned to Finland, while those who stayed sent word back about the United States. Some actively recruited immigrants to come across the Atlantic. One of the earliest of these recruiters was a man named Christian Taftes. He recruited miners—including many earlier Finnish migrants in Norway, followers of Laestadius—and brought them to northern Michigan to work in the Quincy copper mines.

In 1869, Carl Sjödahl (Charles Linn) returned to Finland and recruited 53 Finns, mostly from around Helsinki, to join him in Alabama. Some, according to notices placed in the newspaper *Hufvudstadsbladet*, were young women who were to be placed as maids, mostly in Montgomery, Alabama. Others were men needed to help construct a railroad in the Alabama mountains. They were offered free passage to America and, if they desired it, a free return trip after four years. In these years after the Civil War, the people in this area of the South were apparently trying to use immigrants in jobs formerly done by Black slaves.

Few others seem to have followed in Linn's footsteps to the South. But recruiting for work in the northern United States continued and widened. In the 1870s, an American preacher-recruiter, Josiah Tustin, brought over some dozens of immigrants to work for Michigan firms like the Northern Pacific Company. Many of these, mostly Swedish-speaking Finns, went to Grand Rapids.

Some recruiters, like Swedish-American Hans Mattson, who worked in Gothenburg, Helsinki, and St. Petersburg, distributed printed material designed to entice people to emigrate. Some of them worked for shipping lines, which had long since discovered that there was money to be made from emigrant passages. Often they would gather a party of a few hundred emigrants, from various Scandinavian countries, and guide them across to particular sites in America. In 1873 one such party, including Finns from both Finland and Norway, was put together by agents of the Allan Line. It included a number of Finns, Swedes, and Swede-Finns who were being brought over by a Swedish employment agency in Duluth,

Minnesota. In the same shipload were a large number of Finns who had been working in mines in northern Norway and were being brought over to work in the mines of Hancock, Michigan. Others from this same party dispersed to other cities, including Minneapolis, Chicago, Quebec, and Rockford, Illinois.

Through the 1870s and 1880s, many Finns from the coastal towns were emigrating, joined by increasing numbers from the rural districts. "America fever" continued to spread until, by the beginning of the 1890s, emigrants were coming from all provinces of Finland, though still primarily from around Vaasa and Oulu.

Finnish emigration continued strong until 1893, when a depression in the United States temporarily dampened enthusiasm. Recruiting after that was less successful. Nor was the Russian government so tolerant of recruiting as it had been. In 1907, when a recruiter came looking for emigrants to take over deserted farms in New York State, the attempt was cut short by the government.

Most of these emigrants, especially in the early stages of the emigration, were poor young men off the farms, who had few skills but plentiful strength and endurance. The numbers are not fully clear, because figures were not kept in the earlier decades, and because some of them returned to Finland. Also, Finnish immigrants were classed by American authorities as Russians. But by World War I, as many as 300,000 Finns had arrived in the United States, over two-thirds of them between the mid-1890s and 1914. Among the early Finnish immigrants, three out of four were Swedish-speaking. But after 1870, more and more Finnish-speakers emigrated, until the proportion of Finnish immigrants was almost equally divided between the two languages.

A New Life

Finns found America a worker's paradise, compared to their homeland. At the turn of the 20th century in the United States a good worker could save as much as $300 a year, or about 1,500 Finnish marks; back home he would be lucky to save 200 marks. Women, who generally worked as servants in America, would earn anywhere from $10 to $40 a month, or 600 to 2,500 marks a year above room and board; at home they would have earned not much more than 120 marks a year.

Many Finns found work as loggers in the north country, as here in Wisconsin.
(Library of Congress, Pinchot Collection)

Many Finns were enticed by the ease of obtaining land. It is true that a large farm of, say, 80 to 100 acres in Michigan might cost as much as $2,000 to $3,000. But—at least in the early years—immigrants could buy land at only $6 to $10 an acre, if they were willing to clear it themselves. More than that, they could keep what they earned for themselves. For poor Finns, suffering the double oppression of the Swedish upper classes and the Russian government, this was enormously meaningful. As one Finnish immigrant put it, when urging a friend to come join him on a Michigan farm: "It is not worth your while to stay in Finland. If the gentlemen [aristocrats] leave something for you, the Russians will come and take it from you slowly but surely."

For the Finns of the 19th century, who were still chafing under the use of Swedish in their homeland's schools and government, and the threatened switch to Russian, America also meant the freedom to speak their own language. The same Michigan immigrant commented: "The farming region is replete with schools. You know here we govern ourselves. The Finnish language is heard wherever one goes . . ."

Like other immigrants, Finns countered the feeling of being "strangers in a strange land" by forming their own communities. In places near

Hancock, Michigan, where a large number of Finns came to work in the mines, Finnish place names still abound. Most tended to settle in the north country, where conditions were something like those at home and their working skills would be of use in mining, lumbering, farming, shipbuilding, and fishing.

They tended to some extent to follow their work. Finnish miners were found in places like Minnesota, especially around Duluth, and Virginia, as well as farther west, from Colorado to California. Many of these Finns later turned from mining to farming or lumbering. Because some of the best and cheapest farmland was gone by the time that Finns began arriving in large numbers, many immigrated westward in the process, to the Dakotas. The Pacific Northwest drew fishers, both on the rivers and on the coast. Some of these extended their activities north to Alaska and south to San Francisco and Los Angeles.

By contrast, Finnish factory workers congregated in the industrialized cities. Substantial Finnish communities formed in the smaller cities of New England, notably Worcester and Fitchburg, in Massachusetts. But many also were drawn to larger cities like New York or Chicago. This was true not only for men but also for women. Many Finnish women worked in mills or factories, or were hired as maids and housekeepers in private homes.

Finnish-American Culture

Wherever Finns were found in sufficient numbers, they founded their own schools, churches, and societies, for everything from temperance and religion to music and gymnastics. Using hymnals and Bibles from the old country, the Finnish church was a mainstay in such communities. In the early years, especially, these churches kept alive the Finnish language and traditions, and passed them on to the children. For some decades, these churches were staffed by pastors from the old country, who followed congregations to the New World. They strongly resisted Americanization. As one Finnish-trained pastor put it:

> We desire to be Lutherans of the Finnish language. Why do we become Americanized so rapidly when our Finnish culture, so abundant and rich, can contribute to the cultural enrichment of the United States? The founders earned their daily bread by hard toil. Why should we who are the beneficiaries of their toil and battles neglect our beautiful language?

This Finnish family passed through Ellis Island around the turn of the century. (Photo by Augustus Francis Sherman, National Park Service)

In 1896, the Finnish Lutheran Church of America founded Suomi College, in Hancock, Michigan, the only Finnish-founded college in America. It played a key role in keeping alive Finnish culture, and especially in training pastors for the Finnish Lutheran Church in America. Many Finns belonged to other Lutheran churches, or to other Protestant churches, such as the Methodist, Congregationalist, or Unitarian churches.

The Finnish language and connections were also maintained strongly by the Finnish-language papers that were founded in various parts of the country. The first of these was *Amerikan Suomalainen Lehti* (*The American-Finnish Journal*), a weekly newspaper established in Hancock, Michigan, in 1876 by new immigrant A.J. Muikku. It lasted less than a year, but was followed by many others—more than 350 over the years. For first generation immigrants—those who had been born in Finland—these papers were especially important. It was the main way they got news of the world, and it spread news from home, in a time when mail service was neither swift nor sure. The Finnish-language press also made available to the immigrants a selection of the literature from their homeland.

Some of the Finnish-American papers were church-related, such as the *Amerikan Suometar* (*The American Finn*), founded by the Suomi Synod in 1899, and the *Auttaja* (*Helper*), founded by the National Evangelical Lutheran Church seven years later. Others were political papers, from left-wing papers such as Hancock's socialist journal, *Työmies* (The Worker), or the *Socialist Toveri* (*Comrade*) of Astoria, Oregon, to more moderate or right-wing newspapers, such as *Raivaja* (*Pioneer*).

In religion, politics, and social life, Finns tended to form many small subgroups, rather than unite in one large Finnish community. Perhaps because they had been forced to conform first to Swedish and then to Russian rule in their homeland, Finns seem to have relished diversity in America. So Finns belonged to many Finnish churches, not just one, and focused more on the pastor of their local congregation than on any wider American church network. In politics, too, Finnish communities would form organizations in support of every type of view from right to left. The same went for social groups. Even small communities would often have several different musical societies or gymnastic clubs. Suomi College president Ralph Jalkanen—himself a Finnish-American—has noted that just about the only thing that united Finns in America was their celebration of *Juhannus* (St. John's Day), the traditional midsummer festivities, welcoming the return of longer days, which are so important in all the Scandinavian countries.

Immigrant Problems

As with all immigrants, however, language posed a problem. Many immigrants—like the Finnish pastor quoted above—had come to America with strongly nationalistic feelings. They preferred to maintain their old language and traditions in "Little Finlands" around the United States. They wanted to exercise the freedom to speak and study Finnish—the freedom that to some extent had been denied them in Finland itself. Of course, even they were influenced by the English spoken around them. They gradually came to speak a peculiarly American dialect of Finnish, which American essayist H.L. Mencken called "Finglish."

On the other hand, some of the Finnish-speakers who wanted to Americanize had special difficulty in learning English. This was partly because Finnish is quite unlike the other European languages. Finnish immigrants certainly realized that education was the key to success in the new land, so they swiftly established libraries for their children. But many of them were not so well geared to learn the new language themselves, because they were poor and uneducated. Although most could read and write in Finnish—the Finnish Lutheran Church had seen to that—they had had little formal schooling in Finland, so they were ill-prepared to begin learning a whole new language and culture here, even if they had the time and energy to do so.

This, in turn, posed an economic problem. Finnish immigrants had strength and the will to work. But without the English language, they would get only the poorest-paid jobs, often those too hard or dangerous to be acceptable to workers with other skills at their command. So the desire to keep within a Finnish community was a double-edged sword, cutting some immigrants off from the promise of America's opportunities. This meant not only better jobs but also the practice of democracy—voting and full participation in the whole range of local and national politics. Some came to feel isolated from the larger world and took refuge in alcoholism, the flip side of the temperance movements that have long been common in Scandinavian communities.

Finns were also not so readily and fully accepted as other Scandinavians were in America. The peak Finnish migration was in the first two decades of the 20th century. This was the time of the so-called "New Immigration," mostly of people from southern and eastern Europe, a time when Americans were beginning to react against the flood of immigrants—especially poor, uneducated ones—from abroad. Unlike the Scandinavians of the earlier "Old Immigration," the Finns were seen as part of this new, less welcome group. This made the Finnish immigrants' isolation within the wider American community even stronger. It is perhaps because of this isolation that the Finns as a group had little impact

This young Finn tried to enter America illegally in 1926, two years after the United States had set quotas limiting the number of immigrants allowed to enter. (Photo by Lewis W. Hine, New York Public Library)

on American culture in the early years, even though there were at one time well over 300,000 of them, nearly as many as other more influential immigrant groups at the turn of the century.

Ralph J. Jalkanen suggested that the motto of the early Finnish immigrants might be: "Work, save money, have children, and return to the old country." Many of them did eventually return to the old country. Figures are unclear, but estimates range as high as one-third of all Finnish immigrants. Some of those returnees found themselves in the peculiar position of being nostalgic for America, once they had returned to Finland. One immigrant was so torn by conflicting ties to Finland and America that he went back and forth several times, and finally concluded that he was happy only when on board ship on the way to one or the other!

8

Danish Immigrants in America

The wild prairie seems so barren and strange. It's like a sea. We are just a speck in the middle of a circle that grows or shrinks as the weather changes. On a clear day we can see an almost endless distance.

Johanne Frederiksen, a Danish
immigrant writing in 1911

Danes began coming to America as early as the 17th century, settling in New Amsterdam along with Dutch colonists. One of them, a Dane named Jonas Bronck, who arrived in 1639, bought a large farm from the Native Americans. The price, we are told, was "two rifles, two kettles, two overcoats, two axes, two shirts, one barrel of apple cider, and six gold coins." That land still bears his name, even though it is today a city borough of one and a half million people. It was Bronck's—the Bronx. Jonas Bronck was not alone. About a hundred Danes had immigrated to New Amsterdam by 1675.

Danes had come to America even before the New Amsterdam settlement. True to their Viking heritage, Danish sailors had been among the crew of Henry Hudson's *Half-moon*, when it explored the Hudson River in 1609. Two Danes captained Dutch ships in later explorations of America's East Coast. Danish rulers in 1619 sent an expedition to explore for a Northwest Passage through the Americas to Asia, and claimed the Hudson Bay region as Novia Dania—New Denmark. On the West Coast, Dane Vitus Bering, in the service of the Russians, discovered the Bering Strait, between Asia and North America, in early 1728. He was one of the first Europeans to explore North America from the west, arriving in Alaska in 1741.

Danes who wished to settle in America, however, generally joined parties sent by their near neighbors, the Dutch. These Danes were not only sailors, but also merchants or farmers who had received the required royal permission to immigrate to Dutch colonies.

The first family of Danes—that of Jan Jansen Van Breestede—came to North America in 1636. Others soon followed. One of them, Jochem Pietersen Kuyter, who arrived on the same ship as Jonas Bronck in 1639, was granted 400 acres of land, which today is the area called Harlem in New York City. Some early Danish settlers moved with the Dutch up the Hudson River to Albany, while others joined in a migration westward to New Jersey. One Dane, Andreas Dreyer, was even governor of the Albany colony in 1673 and 1674.

Many of these early Danish settlers adopted Dutch names and habits. For example, Laurens Andriessen was renamed Laurens Van Buskirk, since his house was next to some bushes (*buskene*) near a church (*kirken*). Required by law to belong to the Dutch Reformed Church, these Danes would be punished if they held private services in their own Lutheran faith.

Even so, some Danes remained Lutherans. Later, in 1648, when fellow Lutherans came to the region from Norway and Germany, they established a Lutheran Church. In 1654, with the help of some Dutch Lutherans in Amsterdam, they received a Lutheran pastor, but he was expelled. Not until 1669, five years after the English took the colony and renamed it New York, were the Danish Lutherans able to worship freely with a pastor of their own faith. But they were prosperous enough and religious enough to finally build their own church in 1704, at what is now Broadway and Rector Street in lower Manhattan.

Religion of a different sort would spur many of the later migrations of Danes. In the second quarter of the 18th century, some Danes were converted to the Moravian form of the Protestant religion, which was banned in Denmark until 1771. Converts came to join Moravian settlements then being established in North America. The first group went to a Moravian colony in Bethlehem, Pennsylvania, in 1742. Whole shiploads came, often with Danish captains and crews. Danes and Norwegians were heavily outnumbered by Germans in these Moravian colonies, and soon merged into the general German-American population, as they married others of the Moravian faith.

Danes occasionally came to America from the Danish West Indies, sometimes for an education, sometimes to settle. Hans Christian Febiger, nephew of the Danish governor of St. Croix, traveled widely along the East Coast in 1772, before settling in Boston. His earlier military training was put to good use when he joined George Washington's forces during the Revolutionary War. A leader in battles such as Bunker Hill, Brandywine, Monmouth, and Yorktown, he was dubbed "Old Denmark" by his men. He finished the war as a brigadier general, and later served as treasurer of the state of Pennsylvania.

In the years after the American Revolution, some educated and skilled Danes—teachers, doctors, ministers, merchants, and artisans of various kinds—immigrated to the United States. One of them, Christian Guldager, a prize-winning artist, painted a well-known portrait of George Washington. Their numbers were never very large, but they brought much appreciated skills to the new nation; they generally settled in cities, especially New York. Danes were proud enough of their heritage to spur the founding of a Scandinavian society in 1844—the first in America. Some Danes were pioneers. In 1848 Danish blacksmith Peter Lassen led a party through the Sierra Nevada to northern California, blazing a new route past the mountain that now bears his name: Lassen Peak. But over time the early Danish immigrants gradually merged with the general American population—that is, their language, dress, cooking, and style of life lost their specifically "Danish" flavor, and became simply "American."

Danish Mormons

The next significant wave of Danish migration was also spurred by religion. In 1850, two Mormon missionaries came to Copenhagen, bringing with them the promise of a "paradise in the far-off mountains." Though they attempted to preach to all Scandinavians, they were most successful among the Danes, especially those in the small villages of Jutland. Mormon converts were urged to go to Utah, where their skills and labor were badly needed. So in the coming years, as Marcus Lee Hansen put it, "conversion and emigration were almost synonymous."

The first Danish Mormons left for Salt Lake City in 1852. By 1860, more than 3,000 Danish Mormons had left Copenhagen for America, traveling either from Hamburg or Liverpool. Some received loans from Mormon funds, but most paid for the journey out of their own pockets. Because they traveled together, they were able to get lower rates for accommodations on chartered ships across the Atlantic and for lodgings in port. On their arrival, in either New York or New Orleans, they were met by Mormon agents, who helped them complete the journey to Utah.

In the following decades, other Danes began to immigrate to the United States as well. But Mormons, many of them skilled artisans, still accounted for over one-third of the 13,000 Danish emigrants in the mid-19th century. So it was, in the 19th century, that the territory of Utah had the largest concentration of Danes in the United States.

The trip to Utah was a hard one. Once beyond the Mississippi and Missouri rivers, travelers had to rely on handcarts or ox-drawn wagons for the 1,000-mile crossing to Utah. Sickness was a real danger. In 1854, a party of Danish Mormons, some 680 strong, lost 160 members to cholera at Westport, Missouri, where they were preparing for the journey across the plains. If travelers did not leave early enough in the year, they would meet snow and bitter cold weather in the Rockies, which they had to cross to reach Utah. Some parties of immigrants even found themselves attacked by American settlers along the way because of their religion.

With problems and delays, the journey from Denmark to Utah could take five months, sometimes more. Even after 1869, when steamships and trains made the journey easier, the trip from Denmark to Utah took 27 days or more. Some Mormon immigrants settled short of Utah, in western Iowa and eastern Nebraska.

Once in Utah or Idaho, the Danes did not generally separate themselves from the rest of the Mormons. This was partly because English was the language of Mormonism, and every Danish convert had begun learning English before leaving home. Various Scandinavian Mormons did hold meetings and social events, such as plays or choral groups. Mormon missionaries and agents, traveling back and forth between Utah and Scandinavia, kept immigrants in touch with their homeland, carrying letters and news. But generally the Danes joined with Mormons of other backgrounds in founding towns, churches, and social and political organizations.

Danes led the way in establishing cooperatives in Mormon country, for everything from irrigation—so necessary in the dry country—to self-

defense, in what was still a wild frontier land. Life was hard in the early years. Many Mormons had to live a rough life in dugouts or adobe houses, until they could build more familiar wood-frame houses. Many of the early Danish immigrants were not entirely happy in the Mormon communities and wrote so in their "America letters." Some were unhappy enough to leave Utah for greener pastures. These "backtrailers" settled elsewhere on the Great Plains, notably around Omaha, Nebraska. With such dissatisfaction and less active missionary work, Danish migration to Utah was not quite so heavy in later years—the number was down to 472 in 1873.

Danes to the Midwest

Meanwhile, small numbers of Danes had been immigrating to other parts of the United States from the 1830s on. At first the Danes were so few that they joined with other Scandinavians in establishing Lutheran congregations. But even these few began to send back America letters praising the new land.

Three figures were especially influential. Danish pastor Claus Laurits Clausen, who headed a congregation established largely by Norwegian settlers, wrote many letters printed in Danish newspapers. Lauritz Jacob Fribert, wrote an influential guidebook, *Haandbog for Emigranter til Amerikas Vest*. Rasmus M. Sorenson, a reformer and member of parliament in Denmark, led a party of immigrants to Waupaca, Wisconsin, in 1852. Later returning to Denmark to lecture, he brought two large parties back with him to America. It was largely due to the efforts of these three that Wisconsin in that period had the most Danes of any state in the Union.

Danish Baptists, many of them followers of Lars Jorgensen Hauge, also came to Wisconsin in the 1850s. There they were joined by some Danish Baptists who had settled for a time in Pennsylvania. Word of these settlements reached Denmark. Socialist reformer Mogens Abraham Sumner set up an emigrant office in Copenhagen, and personally conducted at least 13 groups of emigrants across the Atlantic.

The heavily wooded areas around Milwaukee, Green Bay, and Racine, were especially favored by settlers, many of whom worked as dairy and cheese farmers, as they had in Denmark. At one time, Racine claimed to have a larger proportion of Danes among its population than any city in America. The Dania Society, founded in 1867 to aid immigrants and teach them English, continues to exist—even though many Wisconsin Danish-Americans later moved westward, when the open lands of the Great Plains were made available.

Michigan also attracted many Danish settlers, from the 1850s on. Christian Jensen praised the land:

> Here is a limitless forest land which can be bought for next to nothing. The Americans are honest people. The country is ruled by a president, elected for four years. There are good civil courts and many pretty girls. I shall marry one of them.

Jensen was killed in the Civil War, in his first battle as a Union soldier. But others heard and followed. They came to Montcalm County, and to Muskegon, Manistee, and Marquette counties, to cities like Ashland and Grand Rapids. The mines and lumber mills of Michigan's Upper Peninsula were especially attractive. As elsewhere, Danes often joined with other Scandinavians to form church and social organizations.

During the second half of the 19th century many Danes were drawn to Illinois, especially Chicago. In 1850, fewer than 100 Danes had lived in Chicago. But by 1900, the Danish community there numbered some 10,000, the largest in the land. Some parts of the city in the late 19th century even took on a Danish appearance, as George R. Nielsen described, with "blooming plants on window sills, shiny knockers on doors, and white scoured steps."

From the 1860s on, Danish settlers in increasing numbers moved into Minnesota. Lars Jorgensen Hauge, who had led many Danish Baptists into Wisconsin in the 1850s, led them on to Minnesota in 1861. His settlement at Clarks Grove, in Freeborn County, became the largest Danish Baptist community in the country. Other Danish immigrants came to Minnesota, settling their own communities elsewhere in the state.

But it was Iowa that would become "the most Danish of all states." Some Danes had made their way to Iowa in the years before the Civil War, notably to the northeastern town of Cedar Falls. Other Danes come into Iowa in the late 1860s as workers on the Rock Island railroad and later as settlers. Some Iowa towns, such as Elk Horn, were so thoroughly Danish that English was spoken only with outsiders. Even these communities were not unified in all respects, however. The Danish immigrants had brought with them their homeland's sharp religious divisions. So, even in the small towns of rural Iowa, the population would often be split among sharply differing religious groups.

The prairie states had no heavy forests to clear before land could be worked. Even so, the land was not easy to work. It took strong oxen and a specially crafted plow to break up the prairie sod. Low-lying areas often required draining, a laborious job. And prairie-staters, like all Midwestern farmers, faced natural hazards: droughts, blizzards, fire, grasshoppers, and the like. The lack of trees also meant no readily available wood for building homes, so early settlers often had to live in dugouts.

At first farmers could only grow enough to support themselves and their livestock. Later, as they prospered, they began to market their surplus to others. Transportation was very costly, so cattle were initially favored, because they could be herded to market. But when wheat prices dropped sharply in 1878, some farmers began looking toward dairy farming, which many had engaged in back in Denmark. In the 1880s, Danish immigrants brought to the Midwest the cream separator, a new machine that they had seen in action in Denmark. First introduced at Cedar Falls, Iowa, the separator could handle the large amounts of milk generated on Midwestern farms—and would be economical if used jointly by a group of farmers. Drawing on their homeland's traditions, Danes in various parts of the Midwest established cooperative creameries, to which all area dairy farmers would bring their milk.

Later Immigration

In the last half of the 19th century, some 245,000 Danes immigrated to America. That was one-tenth of the total population of their homeland in 1900: 2,450,000. The peak year was 1900, when 11,000 Danes arrived in the United States. Though immigation occasionally dipped, when the

The railroads opened up the vast Western plains for settlement by Scandinavian and other immigrants.
(New York Historical Society, "Across the Continent, Westward the Course of Empire," lithograph by Currier & Ives, New York, 1868)

United States had one of its economic depressions, and during World War I, it continued strong until 1924. At that time the United States passed a law limiting the number of immigrants allowed into the country. As a result of the low quotas, Danes in later years more often went to other countries, such as Canada. Even so, about 363,000 Danes came to the United States between 1820 and 1975—an enormous number from such a small country.

As with other Scandinavian groups, later Danish immigration tended more toward the cities than the country. Many of these immigrants were unskilled or semiskilled people, who went to work as laborers, factory workers, or servants. Less than 20 percent were skilled craftspeople.

Some Danish immigrants attempted to keep their ethnic identity by founding all-Danish rural towns, sponsored by the *Dansk Folkesamfund* (Danish Folk Society). Such groups founded a number of communities,

Both as a writer and as a photojournalist, Danish immigrant Jacob Riis brought to America's attention the terrible condition of the poor, especially children and immigrants.
(Library of Congress)

such as Tyler, Minnesota; Dagmar, Montana; Danevang, Texas; and Solvang, California, which today attracts many tourists to its Danish-style stores and restaurants.

But most Danish immigrants, while they settled at first in the Danish communites of major cities like Chicago, mixed in rather quickly with the wider American community. Later immigrants, who tended to be more skilled and better educated, especially after World War II, entered the mainstream even more quickly.

Danish-American Culture

Early Danes joined with other Scandinavians in churches, schools, social clubs catering to every interest from sports and singing to charity and folk dancing, and fraternal organizations, offering such programs as health insurance. But later, as the numbers of Danes grew, they often formed their own institutions. Dania, founded in Chicago in 1862, was at first open to all Scandinavians, but later became a network of Danish clubs. *Det Danske Brodersamfund* (The Danish Brotherhood) was a fraternity formed in 1866 to provide insurance for Danish war veterans. Other groups, well over 100 of them, have been founded by Danes across the country.

Like other Scandinavians, the Danes had their own papers. The most important of these was *Den Danske Pioneer* (*The Danish Pioneer*), founded in Omaha in 1872 and still operating as a bi-weekly, though shifted to Elmwood, Illinois, in the late 1950s. Christian Rasmussen, the "Danish Newspaper King," published a string of newspapers and magazines in the upper Midwest, and produced many books in Danish and Norwegian at his printing plants. One of his magazines, *Kvinden og Hjemmet* (*The Woman and the Home*), was edited by two Norwegian immigrant sisters; it was published in two editions, one for Danes and Norwegians, the other for Swedes. While these papers were primarily aimed at rural audiences, some other publications, such as New York's *Nordlyset* (*The Northern Light*) and San Francisco's *Bien* (*The Bee*), still published in Los Angeles, were oriented toward better-educated city-dwelling immigrants. Though Danes quickly adopted American ways, groups and publications such as these kept alive their pride in, and ties with, their heritage.

9

Icelandic Immigrants
in America

"Go to America, young men!"

Icelander Gudmundur Thorgrimsen,
speaking in the mid-19th century

Of all the Scandinavian countries, Iceland began sending immigrants to the United States last. Although Icelanders are descended from some of the world's greatest sailors, they were largely cut off from the rest of the world until late in the 19th century. But between 1870 and 1900, many of Iceland's citizens did leave for America, some for the United States, some for Canada. Because they were counted among the Danish immigrants, their number is not exactly clear, but is probably about 15,000, or about one-fifth of the population.

The first Icelandic immigrants were two young men named Thorarinn Haflidason Thorason and Gudmund Gudmundsson. While working as apprentices in Copenhagen in 1851, they—like many Danes—had become converted to the Mormon religion. On their return, they converted some of their fellow Icelanders. In the mid 1850s, 11 of them left to join the Mormon communities in Utah. A few years later nine more came and settled in the Utah town of Spanish Fork. Over the next two decades, these few were joined by others, some Mormons, some Lutherans and Presbyterians.

Other Icelanders learned about America from friends in Europe. As so often happened, one or two people played a key role in the course of

112

emigration. Icelandic merchant Gudmundur Thorgrimsen was host to many international visitors at his home in Eyrarbakki, about 50 miles from Reykjavik. Thorgrimsen lauded the promise of America, and often recommended: "Go to America, young men." One of his Danish clerks, William Wickman, took that advice and in 1865 went to live with relatives in Milwaukee, Wisconsin. Wickman wrote many letters to Thorgrimsen, praising the new land and its opportunities. He offered to help and advise any Icelanders who wished to emigrate.

Four young men took advantage of the opportunity and left to join Wickham on Washington Island, in the northern section of Lake Michigan. As they passed through Reykjavik, many people tried to warn them of dangers ahead. They asserted that immigrants could not even write to friends and relatives in Iceland—or that if they could write, all letters would be read by United States government officials. Others warned of dangers. What if they should be captured and eaten alive by savages, or thrown into slavery? But, trusting in Wickham's letters, the four journeyed to Washington Island.

Soon they and Wickham had founded a proper Icelandic settlement on the island, clearing the land of trees, building log cabins for shelter, fishing in the bountiful waters, and shipping salted fish to market in homemade wooden barrels. Letters quickly began to flow back to Iceland, describing the abundant food: pancakes and syrup, white bread, pork and beans, and, best of all, coffee, Icelanders' favorite drink. These Icelandic-Americans noted that this was only the diet of relatively poor, new immigrants, and that many of their neighbors—especially Norwegians and Germans—ate five times a day. Even their little island, only seven miles long and five miles wide, they asserted, would readily support "even the laziest Icelander with a houseful of children."

Early Settlers

The message was spread widely in Iceland, and soon others began to make their way to America. A party of 15—14 young men and the bride of one of them—left home in June of 1872. As Icelanders were obliged to do, they headed for Europe, sailing to Liverpool and there taking a liner to Quebec, via Halifax, Nova Scotia, and a train to Milwaukee. These were educated young people who had studied English. Using their new language, they had a chance meeting with a German Lutheran pastor in Milwaukee. Some of the small party stayed in Milwaukee, and one of them, Páll Thorlaksson, entered a Lutheran theological seminary nearby, later becoming an important figure in Iceland's religious community. The rest of the party went on to Washington Island. Another seven Icelanders soon joined those in Milwaukee, coming via New York and Castle Garden.

The Icelanders on Washington Island were somewhat disappointed, because there was actually very little land there for them to farm, and the summer working days were much shorter than they had known in Iceland. Their fellow immigrants in Milwaukee entered on a very different kind of life. They rented a house, run by the young bride, and the men went to work in a machine factory—something quite unknown in Iceland.

In the inevitable America letters, other Icelanders heard the message about the new land's opportunities. By 1873, Páll Thorlaksson had been requested to put down a deposit on some land to be settled by 500 Icelanders. He refused, recommending instead that they come work with experienced farmers, to learn the conditions and best working methods for the land. He offered to arrange work for them with farmers in Minnesota and Wisconsin. He arranged for the party, by now 200 strong, to work with Norwegian-American farmers in Wisconsin.

In the end, 165 Icelanders arrived in Quebec in August of 1873. To Thorlaksson's surprise, they were accompanied by a Danish agent employed by the Canadian government. The agent asserted that these Icelanders were Canadian immigrants and promised to give each family 200 acres of land, providing shelter while they were building the necessary houses and barns. Most of the new immigrants followed the Danish-Canadian agent. But 50 went with Thorlaksson to the farms where he had arranged for them to work. There they received a warm welcome from the Norwegian-American farmers.

Some of the single men chose to remain in Milwaukee, joining the work forces of the local factories. They had a hard time in their first year or two. The United States was in an economic depression and jobs were hard to come by. Many young immigrants worked on the docks for a time and then, when winter stopped Great Lakes shipping, took off into the countryside looking for work. But, without any special arrangements by someone like Thorlaksson, many of them were run off farm after farm.

After sleeping outside for weeks in a fruitless search for work, many returned to Milwaukee. There they heard of lumbering work in the Wisconsin forest. Having lived in almost treeless Iceland, these young men had little experience with an axe, but they soon became able lumberjacks, working on the docks in summer and in the woods in winter.

During these difficult early years, Icelanders in Milwaukee stayed in close touch with each other. They even founded a short-lived cultural organization called The Icelandic Society of the Western Hemisphere. Other cultural organizations followed, and kept the Icelandic community together. They were pleased that in 1874 the United States noted with considerable publicity the 1,000th anniversary of the founding of Iceland. Major figures, such as Henry Wadsworth Longfellow, wrote about the event, and direct contacts between America and Iceland increased. On August 2, 1874, the date on which Iceland celebrated this anniversary, the Milwaukee Icelanders arranged their own celebration, in a borrowed Norwegian Lutheran church.

In the same period, some Icelanders began to look elsewhere in North America for a place to settle. They found Wisconsin too hot in summer and too cold in winter, unlike their more temperate maritime homeland. Some looked in Nebraska, Iowa, and elsewhere in Wisconsin. Others, notably Icelandic-American poet and editor Jón Ólafsson, suggested Alaska. With the support of President Ulysses S. Grant, who thought it "desirous to have Alaska settled . . . . by an industrious, hardy people," Ólafsson led a party to explore Alaska as a settlement site. But in the end, nothing came of it. In the years that followed, Canada, with its active recruiting efforts, became the major focus of immigration.

Icelandic-Americans were still trying to find an appropriate place for an Icelandic colony. Those who had originally gone to work for Norwegian-American farmers, now wanted farms of their own. With support from Norwegian and German Lutherans, some settled in a forested area about 150 miles from Milwaukee, near Shawano Lake, Wisconsin. But, though the land is today valued farmland, these Icelanders had neither the tools nor the experience to clear heavily wooded land. This colony came to nothing.

Then in 1875 Icelanders founded their first permanent settlement, in Lincoln and Lyon counties in Minnesota. The first settler, Gunnlaugur Pjetursson, drove a team of oxen from Wisconsin some hundreds of miles north to what is now Minneota, Minnesota.

Canadian Detour

Some of these early immigrants went north to join Icelanders in Canada. They, too, dreamed of an Icelandic colony, and looked westward toward the prairies. In July 1875, they came to Winnipeg, Manitoba, arriving in the midst of a grasshopper plague. This, too, is today prime farm land. But the committee regarded the plague as an ill omen—a sign of God's disfavor, as in the Bible—so they pushed on to Lake Winnipeg. Though the land was flat and marshy, the scouting party was impressed by the abundant fish and the ease of transportation provided by the waterways—no small consideration in the days before the railroads had opened the West.

With strong support from the Canadian government, Icelanders—including some hundreds directly from Iceland—settled a "New Iceland" near Lake Winnipeg. Some of these Icelanders decided to stay in Winnipeg, on the Red River, south of the lake, attracted by good wages on its docks. They founded the largest urban community of Icelanders in North America. The others went on to Lake Winnipeg, to build a small collection of log cabins. They called their colony Gimli, after the paradise in Icelandic myths.

Unfortunately, the Icelanders were totally unprepared for the long and bitter Canadian winter. The lake froze and they had no experience of fishing through holes in the ice. So they were forced to rely on moldy, worm-ridden food from the local trading posts. Many became ill through lack of nutrition; then came a terrible epidemic of smallpox. Not knowing of all these difficulties, hundreds more came from Iceland in the summer of 1875 to join the colony.

In the Dakota Territory

Meanwhile Páll Thorlaksson and others were still hoping to found an Icelandic settlement in the United States. They decided that the Icelanders should settle on some land in the Red River region of the Dakota Territory, in what is now Pembina County, North Dakota, just south of the Canadian border. A number of Norwegian-American and German-Americans—some of the veterans of the Civil War—had already settled there and were willing to help their fellow Northern Europeans establish

On the Great Plains, as here in the Dakota Territory in 1885, early settlers often had to live in sod houses, until they were able to build proper wood-frame houses.
(Photo by J.N. Templeman, Library of Congress)

themselves in the prairie land.

So in the summer of 1878, about 100 settlers from Lake Winnipeg's struggling New Iceland colony began to head southward toward the Dakota Territory. Some of them had spent almost everything they had brought with them from Iceland or earned since; they walked the entire 160 miles. Canadian authorities tried to stop the party and did take some of their goods. They argued that Canada had spent a great deal of money on them, expecting that the Icelanders would settle in Canada permanently. But most of the party pressed on toward their destination. Among the Icelandic pioneers to arrive in the Dakota Territory was an 18-month-old child, Vilhjálmur Stefansson, who would later become an internationally respected Arctic explorer.

This was new land. Custer's Last Stand had taken place west of the Dakotas, in southern Montana, only two years earlier, and the name of Sitting Bull, who was still alive, was well known to the Icelanders. Indeed, on their way to the Dakota Territory, the Icelanders saw a large party of Native Americans and hoped it had no warlike intentions. Restlessness, if not full-scale war, between settlers and Native Americans would continue for some decades, especially during the 1880s when Canada's Riel

Rebellion of Native Americans and mixed-blood people called *métis* kept the northern prairie astir.

Icelanders soon found that the temperature extremes were as great as elsewhere on the northern prairie, but the land was also teeming with plant and animal life. These Dakota settlers were soon joined by many fellow Icelandic-Americans from Wisconsin and Minnesota, and more penniless families from Lake Winnipeg.

The first years were difficult. Severe winters, especially in 1879-80, caused shortages of food and of seed for planting. Many settlers lacked the necessary tools for cultivating the soil and had no money to buy them. The frontier was too new to have any farm banks, and no direct government help was available—the land was, after all, free under the Homestead Act. Many immigrants, too poor to farm their own land, initially worked for others, or worked on the railroads that were pushing westward, until they had enough money to stock and run a farm.

The Icelandic-Americans of the Dakota Territory may have been poor in goods, but they were rich in friends. Norwegian- and German-American settlers in the area generously helped them through the hard early years. Some of the more prosperous Icelandic immigrants mortgaged their livestock and possessions to help provide the necessary provisions for the poorer settlers. Reverend Páll Thorlaksson traveled widely in the Dakotas and Minnesota talking to Norwegian-Americans, many of whom provided either money, in the form of gifts and loans, or livestock on favorable terms, to tide the settlers over during these lean years. That the loans were provided by the Norwegian-Americans and paid back steadily by the Icelandic-Americans cemented the longstanding ties between the two groups.

By the 1880s the Dakota Territory was established as the focus of Icelandic immigration. From then until the decline of Icelandic emigration at the turn of the century, most Icelanders headed directly toward this Icelandic colony. Some Icelanders eventually moved westward to the Pacific Coast, most likely following the Norwegian lead. Some traveled north to join—or rejoin—the Icelandic community that had remained in Canada. But most came to the Dakota Territory and stayed.

Icelandic immigrants soon blended in with the other Dakota settlers. Many of them were Norwegian, with whom the Icelanders shared a history, a language, and a religion. Other Scandinavians, too, were found in the Dakota Territory, along with many Germans and Irish. Though the

Icelanders for a time kept their own language, they soon saw that English was necessary for getting on with their neighbors.

And in a few years, the land began to yield its riches. From their German neighbors, Icelanders learned to plant unfamiliar vegetables such as beets, carrots, and cabbages. They learned to make tasty jams and jellies from the wild fruit that abounded in the region. Icelanders, who had been sheep ranchers for a thousand years in Iceland, raised sheep and other livestock in North Dakota as well. The sheep provided meat and clothing, from both hides and wool. The cows provided milk and cheeses. And Icelander's still relished their favorite drink: coffee.

Icelandic-American Culture

Like other prairie pioneers, Icelanders generally lived in log cabins. These were usually one-story affairs, with a roof of sod, though a more prosperous settler might have a sleeping loft upstairs. The best piece of furniture was often a brightly painted traveling chest brought from Iceland, and hauled around the country since then. Books of sagas and hymns were usually found, even in poor homes, for Icelanders have always had a strong regard for literature. In 1882, when local town governments began to be organized in the region, Icelanders were among the first officeholders.

In the 1880s two Icelandic papers were established in Winnipeg: *Heimskringla* (*The Globe*) and *Lögberg* (*The Tribune*). These were widely circulated in the Icelandic community in North Dakota, and kept the immigrants in touch with each other. The two papers later merged and, 100 years later, the *Lögberg Heimskringla* still had a readership (in both English and Icelandic) of 1,000 in North America and as many in Iceland, subsidized by the Icelandic government. By 1895, Minnesota's Icelandic-Americans had their own paper, *The Minnesota Mascot*, which was also circulated in North Dakota. It was a sign of the times that this paper was published in English, not Icelandic. Icelandic-Americans also read some Norwegian publications, such as *Decorah Posten*, which included serial novels that kept readers spellbound.

Like other Scandinavians, the Icelandic-Americans were divided over one thing: religion. Quite apart from those who had followed English or American forms of religion, such as Mormonism, or Unitarianism, the

Icelandic-American Vilhjálmur Stefansson became a world-famous explorer and expert on the Arctic; he showed how, by using local resources, explorers could spend years north of the Arctic Circle.
(Library of Congress)

Icelandic Lutherans were divided among themselves. Reverend Páll Thorlaksson had joined with the Norwegian Lutheran Synod, which was then closely associated with the rather conservative Missouri Lutheran Synod. But Icelandic-trained Reverend Jón Bjarnason inclined to a more liberal form of Lutheran worship. The Icelandic communities in North America—both in Winnipeg and in North Dakota—split sharply over the two forms of Lutheranism.

Then in 1884, two years after Páll Thorlaksson's death, the Icelandic Lutherans united to form their own synod, based in Winnipeg. This largely united the two sides. And, unlike the church in Iceland, the church in America became the focus of many of the Icelandic-Americans' social activities, through such organizations as ladies' aid societies and young peoples' societies. Choirs, singing both traditional Icelandic music and classical European music, such as chorales by Johann Sebastian Bach, were extremely active in the Icelandic-American Lutheran churches.

Education had always been important to Icelanders. They established their first formal schools in the Dakota Territory in 1881. These schools were conducted in English, and many a parent learned English from their own school-taught children. So Icelandic immigrants prepared to move into the mainstream of American life.

10

The Scandinavian-American Heritage in Modern Times

Another thing that makes me like this country is that I can share in the government. In Sweden my father never had a vote, and my brother never could have voted because there is a property qualification that keeps out the poor people, and they had no chance to make money. Here any man of good character can have a vote after he has been a short time in the country, and people can elect him to any office. There are no aristocrats to push him down, and say that he is not worthy because his father was poor. Some Swedes have become governors of states, and many who landed here poor boys are now very rich . . .

Axel Jarlson, mid-19th-century Swedish immigrant

The Scandinavian immigrants of the early 19th century were sometimes mocked, exploited, or looked down upon by English-speaking Americans. They were called "greenhorns" and were laughed at for their "foreign" language and old-country ways. This was especially true of those Scandinavian immigrants who lived in communities off by themselves, speaking mostly or wholly in their own language. Those who lived in towns and cities, mixing every day at work and in social settings with other people, were more likely to speak English sooner and to become fully accepted by the wider American community.

But whatever reservations English-speaking Americans had about

*Second and third genera-
tion Scandinavian-
Americans, like the
Hedlund family on the
Fourth of July in 1911,
often fully adopted
American ways.*
(Photo by James Pavlicek,
Minnesota Historical
Society)

Scandinavian immigrants were largely swept away in the late 19th century when the so-called "New Immigration" began. From then through the Great Depression of the 1930s, most immigrants came from southern and eastern Europe, and in much larger numbers than the earlier waves of immigration—the "Old Immigration," largely from northern Europe and largely Protestant. In the eyes of English-speaking Americans, these new immigrants were "different." Even though most of them came from that great ethnic mosaic called Europe, they were from different regions, their languages were not so closely related to English, and their religion was different, more often being Roman Catholic, Jewish, or Eastern Orthodox. Many English-speaking Americans felt their way of life was threatened by the hundreds of thousands of "new immigrants."

In the late 19th and early 20th century, Scandinavian immigrants were seen as desirable recruits to the established "American way of life." It became far clearer that the Scandinavians' language, religion, and culture shared roots common with those of many earlier English and Scotch-Irish settlers. Because they were generally White, Anglo-Saxon (or at least closely related to the English stock), and Protestant, they were sometimes called WASPs. As a result, while " new immigrants" were often targets of discrimination—both on entering through Ellis Island and in their new lives in America—Scandinavians were generally welcomed. One exception was the Finns; since their language was different, and they came from what was then Russian territory, they were often classed as "new immigrants," and discriminated against accordingly.

So the way was paved for Scandinavians to move—even faster than in earlier times—into the mainstream of American life. And they did just that.

Moving On

First-generation Scandinavian-Americans—those who had been born in Europe—tended to lead rather traditional family lives in America, especially in rural areas. As in the old country, women were largely confined to the home, with relatively few outside activities. Men generally ruled supreme in the home, but often worked and socialized outside—singing, dancing, acting, sometimes (though the church frowned on it) drinking and playing cards. Children were firmly disciplined, kept out of the way of adults, and sent to work at an early age—except for those who showed a real aptitude for schooling.

In the later years of immigration, many more young single men came to America than families. As they prospered, they looked around them for wives. Some found them in the local Scandinavian community. Then letters would be sent back across the ocean to in-laws they would probably never see. One young Swedish girl wrote to her new parents-in-law:

I must write a few lines and tell you that it is I who have stolen your son, whom you will never get back again, for I want to have him always. . . . We only wish you could come and see us. . . . We have a nice little home with four rooms, and it is very pretty here in the summer, it is almost like at home in Dalsland.

But too few such women were available for the many Scandinavian immigrants seeking wives. Some men found wives outside of the Scandinavian community. But many wrote back for a wife to come and join them—sometimes it was someone they knew from the old country, sometimes they asked friends or relatives to choose a wife for them. Memories of home died hard, and immigrants often reached back for links with the past. One Swedish immigrant, a widower after 14 years in America, wrote this poignant letter to his first girl friend, care of the local pastor:

Dear Anna:

I wonder how you have it and if you are living . . . Are you married or unmarried? If you are unmarried, you can have a good home with me. I have my own house in town and I make over ten *kroner* a day. My wife died last year in the fall and I want another wife. I have only one girl, eleven years old. If you can come to me I will send you a ticket and travel money for the spring when it will be good weather. . . . It is around 24 years since we saw each other. You must wonder who I am. My name is Einar, who worked over at Vensta for Adolf Johanson when you were at Andersons,' and you were my first girlfriend. If you can't come maybe you know somebody else who wants to become a good housewife.

From a pattern of rather large families in the pioneer years, where every extra pair of hands counted, Scandinavians began to have smaller families of two to four children. In all this, Scandinavians were like many of the other immigrants coming to America in the late 19th and early 20th centuries.

And, like them, Scandinavians were constantly subjected to pressure from the wider society to become Americans, and were looked down upon for holding to their old country ways. Those in rural farm areas, or in small communities of fellow Scandinavians, tended to keep their native language the longest—especially the women, who were largely confined to home by their work. Men, who generally had more contact with the wider

Many Scandinavian-Americans stayed on the farm, like this young man who came to work in Montana after his own South Dakota harvest was over. (Photo by Marian Post Wolcott, Library of Congress, Farm Security Administration, 1941)

American community, tended to learn English more quickly; those who lived and worked with other English-speakers in large towns or cities learned English the most quickly.

Of course, some immigrants—especially the young—embraced Americanization, adopting with all possible speed the language and ways of the new land they had chosen. In doing so, they often were able to find more material success than their fellow Scandinavians. But that was frequently at the cost of their ties with their own traditions. Later in life, many found this a very great cost, indeed.

Like other immigrants, Scandinavian-Americans found that the second and third generations—their children and the grandchildren—had minds of their own. Many of them chose to move to the towns. There they often moved into the professions, such as law, engineering, or education, and became prominent and highly respected citizens, active in politics, business, and the social life of the community. In the late 19th and early 20th centuries, they were often joined by fresh immigrants from Scandinavia,

As coach at Notre Dame in the early 20th century, Norwegian immigrant Knute Rockne changed the way football was played by developing such now-standard techniques as the forward pass and the wholesale shift of the defensive line.
(Library of Congress)

skilled, educated people who chose more often to settle in the towns and cities than had the immigrants of earlier times. In the late 19th and 20th centuries, many single young Scandinavian women came to America to work as domestic servants. (Before then, most women came to join their husbands or fiancés).

To the Cities

Though many Scandinavians remained on the land—as their descendants still remain—Scandinavians also began to form large communities in the cities. Substantial Swedish-American populations were found not only in Midwestern cities like Chicago (which, as late as the 1920s, had the third largest Swedish population in the world), Rockford, Minneapolis, St. Paul, Madison, and Duluth, but also in the East, in New York, Brooklyn, Boston, Worcester, Hartford, Jamestown, and Providence. By 1900 over 40 percent of the Swedish immigrant population was settled in the East, and over 26 percent of the total lived in cities.

Among Norwegian-Americans, later generations and new immigrants tended to concentrate increasingly in the Eastern industrial states of New York, Massachusetts, Connecticut, New Jersey, and Pennsylvania, as well as in Illinois and the Pacific Coast states, especially California. By mid-century, New York City alone had over 30,000 Norwegians, more than 20,000 of them in a large Norwegian community in Brooklyn. Chicago, Minneapolis, and Seattle also had large Norwegian populations. But, more than the Swedes, Norwegian-Americans generally preferred somewhat smaller cities and towns.

Danish-Americans continued to be concentrated in Utah, as new immigrants came to swell the Danish population there. After World War II, about 900 Danes immigrated to Utah in just 10 years, between 1945 and 1955. Iowa, called "the most Danish of all the states," also had many Danes. But Danes, more than other Scandinavians, spread widely around the country, and people of Danish descent are to be found in almost every state in the Union.

Even more than their fellow Scandinavians, Danes tended to settle in industrial cities, both large and small. In 1910, the U.S. Census showed almost half of the Danish immigrants living in cities; by 1970, only 4 percent were left on the farms. In the early 20th century, for example, a Perth Amboy, New Jersey, terra-cotta factory employed 5,000 Danes in a town that had no more than 30,000 residents. Racine, Wisconsin; Omaha, Nebraska; and Council, Bluffs, Iowa, continued to have large Danish populations. The West Coast cities, especially Los Angeles, also became home to many Danes. But Chicago attracted the most Danes; at least as recently as the 1930s, it had the largest Danish population of any city outside of Denmark.

Finnish-Americans, too, scattered widely through all the states of the Union, but tended to concentrate in northerly areas. Like the earliest Finnish immigrants, many continued to work as miners or loggers in states like Michigan, Minnesota, Montana, California, Oregon, Wisconsin, and Washington. Finns clustered particularly around Hancock and Marquette, Michigan, and Duluth, Minnesota. In the Pacific Northwest, many worked at fishing or in canning factories, especially around Astoria, Oregon, and along the Columbia River. The mills and factories of Illinois (especially around Chicago), Ohio, and Massachusetts, have also been attractive. Many Finns settled as farmers in the New England states.

North Dakota continued as the home of many Icelandic-Americans. They have been extremely active in the state's politics. But they have also spread far and wide around the country. Though they generally learned English quickly and moved smoothly out into the wider community, they have remained proud of their heritage. So they have founded Icelandic-American organizations to preserve their ethnic traditions and provide cultural activities for their members. Such organizations are found from New York to Alaska and California, in cities such as Washington, D.C., New York, Minneapolis, Chicago, and Seattle. Like other Scandinavians, they tended to leave the farm in the second and third generation. In 1970, over half of the American citizens of Icelandic descent lived in urban, rather than rural, areas.

Wars and Depression

Many Scandinavian-Americans faced painful decisions in a 20th century filled with two world wars and a depression. Their homelands had close ties with Germany, and here in America, Scandinavians and Germans had worked side by side to open much of the Midwest. They lived in the same towns, attended the same schools and churches, and often married across ethnic lines. So, at the approach of World War I, many Scandinavian-Americans were isolationists. Not wanting to fight against Germany, they wanted the United States to stay out of the war. Such a view was unpopular, and probably led to the defeat of Charles A. Lindbergh, Sr., in his bid for the governorship of Minnesota in 1918. His son, aviator Charles Lindbergh, Jr., and some others of Scandinavian descent, faced the same problem in the years approaching World War II. But once Adolf Hitler's true intentions became clear to them, most Scandinavian-Americans wholeheartedly supported the United States war effort. During World War II, Finnish-Americans were especially torn because Germany had been their traditional ally against Russia's unwanted domination. But their traditional ally did nothing when Russia attacked Finland in 1939, and, indeed, Russia took the province of Karelia at the end of the war.

The Great Depression of the 1930s posed a different problem. In that time of national economic collapse, many immigrants found themselves without jobs or money. Those who were unskilled or uneducated or had not overcome the language barrier were often the first to feel the pinch. Some considerable numbers of Scandinavian immigrants returned to their homelands in this period. The figures are not at all clear, but as many as 30 to 40 percent of the Finnish immigrants returned to their homeland during the Depression—perhaps partly drawn by the fact that their land had become independent for the first time in seven centuries. The other Scandinavian groups sent far fewer immigrants back home. Most immigrants, like most Americans, simply rode out the storm.

Building America

Many Scandinavian-Americans worked in trades related to building, woodworking, or engineering. This is not surprising, since many of them had made all or part of their living from the forests in their homelands. Among the unskilled, many worked as loggers and sawyers in woodworking factories. Those who were skilled often worked as carpenters, toolmakers, electricians, contractors, furniture-makers, manufacturers, and industrialists. They worked with automobiles, elevators, railroads, and airplanes, as well as at manufacturing in general. Swedish builders, for example, were active in rebuilding Chicago after the great fire of 1871, and many helped put up the structures for the Chicago Exposition of 1893. Norwegian Ole Singstad engineered New York City's Holland Tunnel, the first tunnel designed for use by automobiles, which opened in 1927. Danish architect and ironworker Niels Poulson handled much of the construction and ornamentation of Grand Central Terminal, which opened in New York City in 1913. He later designed the Lincoln Tunnel and the Queens Mid-town Tunnel as well. Finnish architect Gottlieb Eliel Saarinen came to the United States in 1923, after winning second prize in an international competition to design a new building for the *Chicago Tribune*. He became an internationally famous architect, with many buildings to his credit, as did his son, Eero, who designed the striking TWA terminal at John F. Kennedy Airport in New York City.

Scandinavian-Americans were also active in industry. Danish immigrant William Knudsen became president of General Motors, and was appointed by President Roosevelt to mobilize American industry for war production in World War II. Swedish-American industrialist Vincent Bendix invented a self-starter for automobiles, eliminating the hand-cranks previously used, and later developed a major manufacturing corporation, popularly known for its household appliances. His countryman, Harold Bostrom, developed the first molded bucket seats for automobiles, and Swedish-American George Eastman the first handheld camera. Norwegian-American Ole Evinrude gave America its popular outboard motor. Norwegian-American Conrad Hilton built an international chain of hotels, while his countryman Arthur Anderson founded one of the nation's most respected accounting firms.

During World War II, Norwegian immigrant Edward Groe put his mechanical skills to use making airplane motors, instead of electric organs.
(Photo by Ann Roesner, Library of Congress, Office of War Information, July 1942)

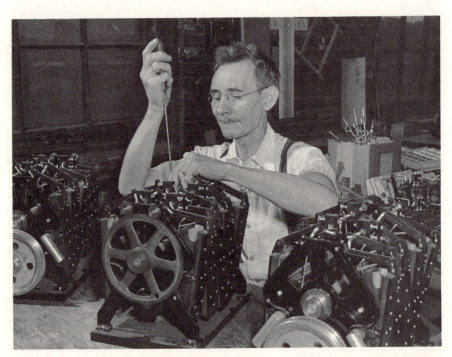

For his work in nuclear chemistry and atomic energy, Swedish-American Glenn T. Seaborg received the Nobel Prize and, here, the Legion d'Honneur *from the French ambassador.*
(Copyright *Washington Post*; reprinted by permission of the D.C. Public Library)

Scandinavian-Americans were found on the "cutting edge" in many fields. Swedish-American geologist Johan August Udden developed some of the analytical techniques that allowed the full opening of America's oil fields, especially in Texas. Swedish-American Charles A. Lindbergh, Jr., became the first person to fly solo across the Atlantic from America to Europe. Norwegian-American biochemist Conrad Elvehjem discovered a cure for the once-feared vitamin-deficiency disease, pellagra. Norwegian-American Ernest O. Lawrence invented the cyclotron, for which he received the Nobel Prize, an international award founded by Swedish inventor Alfred Nobel. Swedish-American Glenn T. Seaborg won a Nobel prize for his work in nuclear chemistry and served for a decade as chairman of the U.S. Atomic Energy Commission. Icelandic-American explorer and writer Vilhjálmur Stefansson added much to the world's knowledge of the Arctic. Swedish-American Buzz Aldrin even made it into space as an astronaut. Norwegian-American agricultural researcher Norman E. Borlaug was awarded the 1970 Nobel Peace Prize for his work in developing new strains of disease-resistant, high yield grains; the resulting "green revolution" helped ease hunger around the world. Even those Scandinavian-Americans who stayed on the farm were often forward-looking and quick to adopt electricity and other laborsaving devices.

Political Life

Many Scandinavian-American immigrants had come to America with ideals of socialism and cooperation, and many continued to work for these ideals in America. Throughout the country, from Maine to Alaska, Scandinavian-American communities set up cooperatives, ranging from creameries to canneries. Many immigrants were active in socialist or workers' organizations, or worked in labor organizations, especially in industrial areas. Swedish-American Mary Anderson, for example, was a local president in the International Boot and Shoe Workers Union, near Chicago, and helped found the National Women's Trade Union League. Swedish-American Joe Hill—born Joel Hägglund, but Americanized to Joseph Hillstrom—was active in the IWW (Industrial Workers of the World), writing many labor songs, including "Casey Jones." When he was executed in Utah in 1915 after conviction on a flimsy murder charge, he became a labor martyr, celebrated in the popular song, "Joe Hill."

Once in America, most Scandinavian immigrants joined American mainstream parties, while keeping their ideals of a better life. From the Civil War era on, the Republican party—the party of Lincoln—drew most Scandinavians. Many Scandinavians, especially Swedes, voted heavily for prohibition—not surprising, since missionaries of the American Temperance Movement had sparked some of the 19th-century Swedish religious movements. Some Scandinavians broke away in the late 19th and early 20th centuries, being unhappy with the big business orientation of the Republican Party. But not until the Great Depression and Franklin Delano Roosevelt did Scandinavian-Americans split more evenly between Republicans and Democrats.

Wherever they lived, Scandinavians were active in political life. They

Danish immigrant William Knudsen (with bow tie), president of General Motors, tours a plant as President Roosevelt's director of war production in World War II.
(Library of Congress)

were mayors, sheriffs, lawyers, judges, and representatives of all sorts. Many moved on to higher state and federal offices. In North Dakota alone, the tiny Icelandic community gave at least three attorneys general, three state supreme court judges, and a dozen state legislators. Danish immigrants or their descendants have served as governors in at least seven states: Minnesota, Wyoming, South Dakota, Iowa, New Jersey, California, and Nebraska. Two longtime congressmen—Ben Jensen of Iowa and Lloyd Bentsen of Texas—are also of Danish extraction. Swedish-American Charles A. Lindbergh, Sr., was a member of the U.S. House of Representatives for Minnesota, and at least three other Swedish-Americans have served as governor of that state. In 1919, Norwegian-American Congressman Andrew Volstead introduced the ill-fated act prohibiting the sale of liquor. Norwegian-American Karl Rölvaag, son of author Ole Rölvaag, was governor of Minnesota. Since 1895, Minnesota has had at least one senator of Scandinavian ancestry sitting in Congress. Norwegian-American Earl Warren served as governor of California for 10 years and then as Chief Justice of the United States Supreme Court from 1953 to 1969. And two vice presidents of the United States—Hubert Humphrey and Walter Mondale, both of Minnesota—have had Norwegian ancestry.

Intellectual Life

Many Scandinavians also moved into the universities, teaching a wide range of subjects. Some taught Scandinavian languages and literature, as those subjects were granted academic status, first at Minnesota State University in 1883 and at the University of North Dakota in 1891. Norwegian-American Thorstein Veblen was a highly respected and influential economist. Danish-American Martha Elizabeth Petersen became president of Barnard College in New York City. A number of Scandinavian-Americans—true to their farming backgrounds—became experts in various branches of biology and agricultural engineering, making major contributions to the productivity of American agriculture. In the area of sports, Norwegian-born Knute Rockne became a legendary coach at Notre Dame, changing the game of modern football.

Scandinavian-Americans have also been influential in the news media—no surprise, given their high literacy rate and the large number of Scandinavian-language newspapers. Norwegian-American Victor Lawson for a long time ran the *Chicago Daily News* and helped found the news wire service, the Associated Press. Danish immigrant Jacob A. Riis was a crusading journalist with the *New York Tribune* and the *Evening Sun*; his works on the condition of the poor, especially of immigrants and children, helped bring about major social changes. Because of the powerful photographs he took to accompany his work, he is sometimes known as the first photojournalist. The character "Hildy" in the play *The Front Page* was based on an actual Swedish-American crime reporter, Hilding Johnson, who worked for the *Chicago Tribune* in the early 20th century. Eric Sevareid, longtime news analyst for CBS, is of Norwegian background, while columnist Jack Anderson is of Swedish descent. And millions of tourists have found their way around New York with the aid of maps made by Swedish-American Andrew Hagstrom.

Artistic Life

In literature, Swedish-American Carl Sandburg, poet of the diversity and humanity of American life and biographer of Lincoln, is perhaps the best-known artist of Scandinavian descent. Works like *The People, Yes* give an unparalleled picture of the experience not just of Scandinavian immigrants, but of all immigrants. He is far from alone. Kathryn Forbes' recollections of her childhood in a Norwegian-American family in San Francisco formed the basis of the ever-popular play, *I Remember Mama*, celebrating the fortitude and resourcefulness of her mother, facing a new world. Norwegian immigrant Ole Rölvaag wrote powerful novels of immigrant life in the American Midwest, which have won worldwide acclaim. A more recent Swedish immigrant, Paul Erdman, is noted both as an economist and a novelist. And Danish-American Peter Matthiessen has written numerous original works in natural history and social analysis.

Scandinavian-Americans have also been active in the arts. Jenny Lind, the "Swedish Nightingale," took the country by storm when she visited briefly in the 1850s. Sweden has also sent a number of fine opera singers to America—although at the height of Caruso's fame, some gave themselves Italian names. So Swede Harald Lindau became Arnoldo Lindi. Also of Swedish ancestry was Howard Hanson, composer and director of the Eastman School of Music. Danish-American sculptor Gutzon Borglum conceived and created the enduring images on Mount Rushmore; his son, Lincoln, continued the work until his own death.

Swedish-American actress Myrna Loy, still a beauty in her 60s, entertained wounded Vietnam War soldiers in Washington in 1966. (Copyright *Washington Post*; reprinted by permission of the D.C. Public Library)

In the movies, Scandinavian-Americans have been among the most beautiful and glamorous women Hollywood ever produced: Norwegian-American Celeste Holm and Swedish-Americans Greta Garbo, Gloria Swanson, Ingrid Bergman, Myrna Loy, Anna Q. Nilsson, Ann-Margret, and Candice Bergen. Norwegian-born Liv Ullmann is a more recent immigrant. Among the men are two Swedish-Americans: Edgar Bergen (creator of Charlie McCarthy and father of Candice) and Hollywood's favorite Charlie Chan—actually Warner Oland, born Johan Verner Olund. James Cagney, James Arness, and Peter Graves are all actors with Norwegian ancestry. Danish immigrant Frederick Brisson was a highly successful film and theater producer.

The descendants of the Scandinavian immigrants have, in truth, contributed to every aspect of American life. The true extent of their contribution is difficult to assess, since they have so fully moved into the mainstream of American life.

Rejection and Revival

Like many other immigrant groups, Scandinavian-Americans experienced a wide "generation gap" between the first and later generations. The first generation—the original immigrants—often held to their old language and ways of life, while the second generation, their children, generally spoke English as their primary language and adopted American ways. The second generation, sometimes the third, often rejected their parents' way of life. In their eagerness to be fully "American," many cut their ties with the ethnic traditions of their people. The process showed itself in many of the Scandinavian institutions. Churches, private schools, newspapers, social clubs, and fraternities founded by immigrants had often conducted their activities in their native language. But in the 20th century, the size of such groups began to decline, for there were fewer Scandinavian-speaking immigrants to keep up the membership and the newer generations wanted to speak only English. Then, such groups either disbanded, merged with other similar groups, or adopted English as their working language. The language of Icelandic Lutheran churches, for example, was predominantly Icelandic into the 1930s, when English began to take over. That pattern was found all over the country. It was sped by the two world wars, when American feeling ran strongly against "hyphenated" Americans. It was in these decades that many of the churches, for example, dropped the designation "Norwegian" or "Danish" and became simply "Lutheran" or "Methodist."

Of course, not all of those in the later generations rejected their Scandinavian roots. Some of them kept alive their heritage by studying in one of the Scandinavian colleges. Suomi College, in Hancock, Michigan, for example, allowed Finns a place in which to study both the language and the culture of their ancestors' homeland. Such knowledge came to be very valuable during World War II, when Finland was once again caught in the middle during somebody else's war, between Nazi Germany and the Allies, including the United States and Russia, Finland's perennial foe. Then the United States Army needed to teach Finnish to soldiers who might be sent to fight there.

The situation changed somewhat for many in the third and later generations. Often they wanted to recapture their Scandinavian heritage. The decades after World War II saw a considerable ethnic revival, with Americans showing an increasing interest in their roots. Some studied formally in Scandinavian studies programs in colleges and universities around the country. Then the old immigrant publications were eclipsed by academic studies of immigrant history. Many of these studies were produced by local, state, and national ethnic history associations—such as the Norwegian-American Historical Association, founded in 1925—and then published by university presses, such as the University of Minnesota Press.

Other Scandinavian-Americans revived their interest informally. They visited their ancestors' homeland, read books about their heritage, studied the culture's traditional arts and crafts, and formed groups with others of similar background and interest. Although many of the older immigrant-founded organizations still existed, later generations often founded their own groups.

The homelands, too, were eager to strengthen ties with their American cousins. In the 20th century, numerous organizations have been set up, both in America and in Scandinavia, to collect material on the great waves of immigration to America. Some Scandinavians actively reach out to their American kin through publications. An organization called *Dansk Samvirke* (The Association of Danes Abroad), founded in Copenhagen in 1919, publishes a newsletter to its 7,000 members worldwide, including over 700 in the United States.

Walter Mondale, shown here in 1977 with his wife, Joan, was one of two Americans of Norwegian descent to serve as Vice President of the United States. (Copyright Washington Post; reprinted by permission of the D.C. Public Library)

But even while this was happening, many of the old Scandanavian-American city communities were fading into history. In the decades following World War II, Scandinavian-Americans in urban areas joined with millions of other Americans in the historic move from the inner cities out to the suburbs. Many of the old Scandinavian urban neighborhoods passed largely into the hands of newer or poorer immigrants, such as Latin Americans or Blacks from the South. In Chicago, for example, Scandinavian-Americans had clustered for decades in communities mostly north of the river, near the Loop. But in recent decades, as they prospered, they moved south of the river and out toward the suburbs.

For most Scandinavian-Americans, the long process of "Americanization" is now largely complete. In the suburbs, they no longer gather with others of Scandinavian background, but blend in with the general American population. In some largely rural areas, clusters of Scandinavian-Americans still remain, keeping alive some of the traditional heritage. But decades of radio, movies, and television, of automobiles and airplanes, have meant that no community is much cut off from the wider American population. So, proud as they are of their background, most Scandinavian-Americans have long since dropped the hyphen—and become simply "Americans." And their contributions to the United States are as great and diverse as the nation itself.

Suggestions for Further Reading

General

Babcock, Kendric Charles. *The Scandinavian Element in the U.S.* New York: Arno and the New York Times, 1969; reprint of 1914 edition by the University of Illinois at Urbana.

Derry, T.K. *A History of Scandinavia: Norway, Sweden, Denmark, Finland, and Iceland.* Minneapolis: University of Minnesota Press, 1979.

Evjen, John O. *Scandinavian Immigrants in New York, 1630-1674.* Minneapolis: K.C. Holter, 1916.

Fuhlbruegge, Irene, ed. *The Swedes and Finns in New Jersey.* Bayonne, New Jersey: Jersey Printing Company, 1938. Part of the Federal Writers' Project.

Furer, Howard B., compiler and ed. *The Scandinavians in America*: 986-1970: *A Chronology and Fact Book.* Dobbs Ferry, New York: Oceana Publications, 1972. No. 6 in the Ethnic Chronology series.

Hansen, Marcus Lee. *The Atlantic Migration: 1607-1860: A History of the Continuing Settlement of the United States.* Cambridge, Massachusetts: Harvard University Press, 1945.

Malberg, Carl. *America Is Also Scandinavian.* New York: Putnam, 1970.

Miller, Wayne Charles. *A Comprehensive Bibliography for the Study of American Minorities*, in two vols. New York: New York University Press, 1976.

Nelson, O.N. *History of the Scandinavians and Successful Scandinavians in the United States*, in two vols. Minneapolis: by the author, 1893-1897; reprint, New York: Haskell House, 1969 from 1904 ed. Part of American History and Americana series.

Taylor, Philip A.M. *The Distant Magnet: European Emigration to the U.S.A.* New York: Harper & Row, 1971.

Thernstrom, Stephan. *Harvard Encyclopedia of American Ethnic Groups.* Cambridge, Massachusetts: Harvard University Press, 1980.

Danes

Bille, John H. *A History of the Danes in America*. Madison, Wisconsin: Academy of Sciences, Arts, and Letters, 1896; reprint, San Francisco: R & E Research Associates, 1971.

Evold, Bent. *They Came to America*. Mankato, Minnesota: Creative Education, 1982. Translated from the Danish and edited by J.R. Christianson and Birgitte Christianson. Part of the Dream of America series.

Hale, Frederick, ed. *Danes in North America*. Seattle: University of Washington Press, 1984.

Hvidt, Kristian. *Flight to America: The Social Background of 300,000 Danish Emigrants*. New York: Academic Press, 1975.

————. *The Westward Journey*. Mankato, Minnesota: Creative Education, 1982. Translated from the Danish and edited by J.R. Christianson and Birgitte Christianson. Part of the Dream of America series.

Nielsen, George R. *The Danish Americans*. Boston: Twayne (G.K. Hall), 1981. Part of the Immigrant Heritage series.

Finns

Engle, Eloise. *The Finns in America*. Minneapolis: Lerner Publications, 1967. Part of the *In America* series.

Hoglund, Arthur William. *Finnish Immigrants in America, 1880-1920*. Madison: University of Wisconsin Press, 1960.

Jalkanen, Ralph J., ed. *The Finns in North America: A Social Symposium*. Hancock, Michigan: Michigan State University Press for Suomi College, 1969.

Kero, Reino. *Migration from Finland to North America in the Years between* the United States Civil War and the First World War. Turku, Finland: Turun Yliopisto, 1974.

Kolehmainen, John I. *The Finns in America: A Bibliographical Guide to Their History.* Hancock, Michigan: Finnish American Historical Library, Suomi College, 1947.

Louhi, Evert A. *The Delaware Finns: or, The First Permanent Settlements in Pennsylvania, Delaware, West New Jersey and Eastern Part of Maryland.* New York: Humanity Press, 1925.

Wargelin, John. *The Americanization of the Finns.* Hancock, Michigan: The Finnish Lutheran Book Concern, 1924.

Wuorinen, John Henry. *The Finns on the Delaware, 1638-1655: An Essay in American Colonial History.* New York: Columbia University Press, 1966; reprint of 1938 ed.

Icelanders

Beck, Bennett A. "Icelandic Anniversity in North Dakota." *American-Scandinavian Review*, 41 (Autumn 1955), 245-249.

Bjornson, Valdimar. "Icelanders in the United States." *Scandinavian Review*, 64 (1976): 39-41.

Jackson, Thorstina. "Icelandic Communities in America: Cultural Backgrounds and Early Settlements." *Journal of Social Forces*, Nos. 1-4 (1924-1925), 680-686.

———. "The Icelandic Community in North Dakota: Economic and Social Development, Period 1878-1925." *Journal of Social Forces, No. 5 (1925-1926).*

Stefansson, Vilhjálmur. *Iceland: The First American Republic.* Garden City, New York: Doubleday, 1939; reprint, Westport, Connecticut: Greenwood Press, 1971.

Walters, Thorstina. *Modern Sagas: The Story of the Icelanders in North America.* Fargo, North Dakota: North Dakota Institute for Regional Studies, 1953.

Norwegians

Andersen, Arlow W. *The Norwegian-Americans*. Boston: Twayne (G.K. Hall), 1975. Part of the Immigrant Heritage of America series, Cecyle S. Neidle, ed.

Anderson, Rasmus B. *The First Chapter of Norwegian Immigration 1825-1840: Its Causes and Results*. Madison, Wisconsin: n.p., 1896.

Bjork, Kenneth O. *West of the Great Divide: Norwegian Migration to the Pacific Coast, 1847-1893*. Northfield, Minnesota: Norwegian-American Historical Association, 1958.

Blegen, Theodore C. *Grass Roots History*. Minneapolis: University of Minnesota Press, 1947.

——, ed. *Land of Their Choice: The Immigrants Write Home*. Minneapolis: University of Minnesota Press, 1955.

——. *Norwegian Migration to America, 1825-1860*. Northfield, Minnesota: Norwegian-American Historical Association, 1931.

——. *Norwegian Migration to America: The American Transition*. New York: Haskell House, 1969; reprint of 1940 ed.

Haugen, Einar I. *The Norwegians in America: A Student's Localized History*. New York: Teachers College Press, 1967. Part of the Localized History Series.

Hillbrand, Percie V. *The Norwegians in America*. Minneapolis: Lerner Publications, 1967. Part of the *In America* series.

Lovoll, Odd S. *The Promise of America: A History of the Norwegian-American People*. Minneapolis: University of Minnesota Press, 1984.

Norlie, Olaf M. *History of the Norwegian People in America*. Minneapolis: Augsburg, 1925.

Qualey, Carlton C. *Norwegian Settlement in the United States*. Northfield, Minnesota: Norwegian-American Historical Association, 1938; reprint, New York: Arno Press and the New York Times, 1970. Part of The American Immigration Collection-Series II.

Rosdail, J. Hart. *The Sloopers: Their Ancestry and Posterity*. Broadview, Illinois: Norwegian Slooper Society of America, 1961.

Semmingsen, Ingrid. *Norway to America: A History of the Migration*. Minneapolis: University of Minnesota Press, 1978. Translated from the Norwegian by Einar Haugen.

Wefald, Jon. *A Voice of Protest: Norwegians in American Politics, 1890-1917*. Northfield, Minnesota: Norwegian-American Historical Association, 1971.

Swedes

Ander, Oscar Fritiof. *The Cultural Heritage of the Swedish Immigrant: Selected References*. Rock Island, Illinois: Augustana Historical Society, 1956.

Barton, H. Arnold, ed. *Letters from the Promised Land: Swedes in America, 1840-1914. Minneapolis, Minnesota: University of Minnesota Press for the Swedish Pioneer Historical Society, 1975.*

Benson, Adolph B. The Will to Succeed: Stories of Swedish Pioneers. Stockholm, Sweden: Bonniers, 1948.

Benson, Adolph B., and Naboth Hedin. *Americans From Sweden*. Philadelphia: Lippincott, 1950. Part of the Peoples of America series.

——. *Swedes in America, 1638-1938*. New Haven: Yale University Press, 1938.

Clay, Jehu Curtis. *Annals of the Swedes on the Delaware*. Chicago: Swedish Historical Society of America, 1914.

Hillbrand, Percie V. *The Swedes in America*. Minneapolis: Lerner Publications, 1966. Part of the *In America* series.

Janson, Florence E. *The Background of Swedish Immigration, 1840-1930*. Chicago: Chicago University Press, 1931.

Johnson, Amandus. *The Swedes in America, 1638-1938*, in four vols. Philadelphia: Lenake, 1914; reprint, Philadelphia: Swedish Colonial Foundation, 1953.

——. *Swedish Contributions to American Freedom, 1776-1783*, in two vols. Philadelphia: Swedish Colonial Foundation, 1953-1957.

——. *Swedish Contributions to American National Life, 1638-1921*. New York: Committee of the Swedish Section of America's Making, 1921.

——. *The Swedish Settlements on the Delaware, 1638-1664: Their History in Relation to the Indians, Dutch and English*, in two vols. New York: Appleton, 1911. Reprinted in one vol., *The Swedes on the Delaware, 1638-1664*. Philadelphia: International, 1927; reprint, New York: Burt Franklin, 1970.

Hokanson, Nels Magnus. *Swedish Immigrants in Lincoln's Times*. New York: Harper, 1942. Introduction by Carl Sandburg.

Leiby, Adrian. *The Early Dutch and Swedish Settlers of New Jersey*. Princeton, New Jersey: Van Nostrand, 1964.

Lindberg, John S. *The Background of Swedish Emigration to the United States: An Economic and Sociological Study in the Dynamics of Migration.*

Minneapolis: University of Minnesota Press, 1930; reprinted by Jerome S. Ozer, 1981. Part of the American Immigration Library, Facsimile Reprint Collection.

Nelson, Helge Magnus Oskar. *The Swedes and the Swedish Settlements in North America*, in two vols. New York: Bonnier, 1943.

Runblom, Harald, and Hans Norman, eds. *From Sweden to America: A History of the Migration*. Minneapolis: University of Minnesota Press, 1976.

Thomas, Dorothy Swaine. *Social and Economic Aspects of Swedish Population Movements, 1750-1933*. New York: Macmillan, 1941.

Index